Strike the Right Chord

The Emerging Leader's Guide to
Exceptional Performance

by

DR. MICHAEL BRENNER

Strike the Right Chord
The Emerging Leader's Guide to Exceptional Performance
by Dr. Michael Brenner

For more information or to place bulk orders, contact the author or the publisher at info@skillbites.net

ISBN: 978-1-952281-66-2 eBook
ISBN: 978-1-952281-84-6 paperback

Table of Contents

———— ❦ ————

Dedication

———— ✦ ————

This book is dedicated to my parents, Marty and Brenda,
My sister Laura and brother-in-law Tom,
And my wife Subhi and daughter Nadhi.

Introduction

The concept of this book was inspired by jazz trumpet great Wynton Marsalis's 2004 book, *To a Young Jazz Musician: Letters from the Road.* As a huge fan of jazz and a professional saxophonist, I find myself regularly coming back to this distinctive music — as well as the wisdom of practitioners like Marsalis — for deep lessons on life, work, self-awareness, cooperation, leadership, commitment, tenacity, and freedom. I found *To a Young Jazz Musician* particularly thoughtful in this regard, and its unusual format especially engaging. The book is comprised of a series of letters Marsalis wrote to a young jazz musician named Anthony while the trumpeter was on tour with his band in the early 2000s. Although Marsalis was only 41 at the time of publication, his words suggest a much older soul — one that is optimistic and hopeful despite suffering quite a few bumps and bruises along the way.

As I read Marsalis's book, I realized there are a lot of "Anthonys" in the workplace — so-called "emerging leaders" looking for guidance and support. These capable, ambitious, smart, confident men and women may possess drive and ambition but lack real-world experience simply because they haven't been in the workplace for very long.

That's one of the reasons I decided to write this book. In my 20+ year career in leadership development and consulting, I've met many individuals who accept the mantle of "leader" yet appear to be unaware of just what the role entails. They assume their technical skills as marketers, salespeople, account managers, human resources coordinators, engineers, nurses, educators, etc. will be sufficient to lead others well. Demonstrating competence at your job is obviously a prerequisite for any leader. After all, we're much more likely to follow someone whom we believe is knowledgeable, capable, and experienced. However, they soon discover that *truly effective* leadership requires honing a *different* set of skills.

When it comes to leading others, "competence" extends beyond your ability to simply execute your job responsibilities. It also means being reliable, decisive, empathic, and a good team player. Research suggests your interpersonal skills are just as important as your technical skills—if not *more* important—for successful leadership. These skills, commonly referred to as "soft skills," are meant to stand in contrast to the "hard" skills associated with job-related competencies, e.g., computer skills, analytical skills, project management skills, and so on. Frankly, I've never liked the term "soft skills" and don't typically use it because "soft" implies "easy."

Believe me, mastering *these* skills is anything but easy.

In fact, whenever I ask my clients what their biggest challenges are, their responses almost always involve "soft skills" such as communication, conflict management, trust building, teamwork, and motivating employees. Hardly any ever mention the so-called "hard" skills associated with the technical aspects of their jobs.

Writing a book for emerging leaders is one thing; making it simple, succinct, and honest is quite another. Hundreds of books, articles, research studies, blog posts, webinars, panel discussions, YouTube videos, TED talks, podcasts, and workshops on leadership are churned out each year. Most are worthwhile, but, in my opinion, many are just too complicated. Who has time to read a lengthy book on leadership these days, especially one filled with charts, tables, models, and dense theory? On the other hand, many are too basic. Business fables, for example, are fun to read and may contain a notable lesson or two, but often fall short of capturing the complexity that is a hallmark of today's organizations.

My goal in writing this book was to explore the "sweet spot" somewhere between the two extremes. The best way to do that was to avoid writing yet another conventional book on leadership; instead, I turned to Marsalis's book for inspiration. While I didn't borrow his letter format, I did adopt his candid, introspective, and informal tone. I wrote each chapter as a jazz musician might improvise a solo, starting with a general idea of what I wanted to say and then letting my thoughts take me on a spontaneous journey. I think the result is a narrative that reads more like a conversation than a lecture, just like a good jazz performance!

I want to review a few more items before we get started. Although this book is intended for emerging leaders, i.e., individuals who have been recently hired or promoted into a leadership role, I'm confident more experienced leaders will also find it worthwhile. It's also important to remember that the keys to being a great leader can't be found in any single book, webinar, TED talk, or podcast. Not even this one. The keys lie *within you* and your desire to make a positive difference in people's lives.

OK, let's do this!

A Personal Note

So, you just landed a leadership position in your organization. Congratulations! You no doubt earned it through your perseverance and dedication.

Now the hard work begins.

You see, when most people think about becoming a leader, they tend to think first about all the cool stuff that comes along with the role (and by "cool stuff" I mostly mean a bump in salary and the increased respect that people tend to show you). Isn't that what we celebrate most when it comes to leadership?

Taken to an extreme, we may view the most financially successful leaders as veritable rock stars, envying their yachts, mansions, and Lamborghinis. As with professional athletes, Hollywood actors, and TV personalities, we may look at them and crave to be one of the "beautiful people."

Because only a handful of well-known leaders ever attract the media spotlight, much of what we know (or *think* we know) about leadership is filtered through a lens of obscene wealth. To further foster this perspective, shows like *Shark Tank* equate success with affluence. Those snarky judges weren't selected to crush people's dreams because they're necessarily good leaders. They're there because *they've made a lot of money in business*, both for themselves and for their respective companies and stakeholders.

I know what you're thinking: Folks like Jeff Bezos, Mark Cuban, Lori Greiner, and Elon Musk *must* be good leaders, right? Isn't their fame and wealth direct evidence of good leadership? Yes, but only if you think the size of a person's bank account is direct evidence of their effectiveness as a leader. I don't and never have. Frankly, you shouldn't either.

Don't get me wrong. I'm not saying the success these celebrity businessmen and women have enjoyed is a bad thing or that they're *not* good leaders. I'm simply suggesting that *being* a good leader entails much more than simply making money. There is no shortage of lousy leaders who make money, sometimes a great deal of it. If that's all you have your sights set on, you *may* get rich, but money alone won't *automatically* make you a good leader.

So, what is leadership *really* about?

Are You Making Other People Sound Good?

"Value" means many things to many people. Some view it as the amount of money we make for our organizations. Others see it as the extent to which we help others or contribute to the daily operation of the business. All these perspectives have merit, but when I first started out in this field, I wanted a crystal-clear definition of "value" that applied to leadership: What value do great leaders fundamentally bring to their organizations other than financial?

I found the answer right where I find a lot of inspiration: the world of music.

In the book *Conversations With Great Jazz and Studio Guitarists* by Jim Carlton, there is an interview with Los Angeles–based guitarist Barry Zweig. Carlton asks Zweig to share an overview of the gigs he's played in the last few days. Zweig's response includes one of the most on-point descriptions of leadership I've ever come across:

> I know my role as a guitarist in a rhythm section. The basic role of a guitarist is to be a good accompanist. That's what makes your value: making other people sound good. The Golden Rule really applies in a rhythm section: what would you like to have going on behind you? You want somebody listening to you. Listening is the whole thing. Be there for that person and pay attention. Just get underneath and don't play anything to take away from their moment. That's it.

Zweig's quote inspired me to jot down the following Five Critical Responsibilities of Leaders:

1. Make other people sound good.
2. Pay attention to what's going on "behind" you.
3. Listen with sensitivity.

4. Provide support and encouragement.
5. Don't steal the spotlight from others or step on their toes.

Of course, there's more to leadership than these five items. Leadership encompasses a wide array of behaviors including building trust, communicating clearly, solving problems, getting work done, handling conflict, and navigating change. We'll discuss many of these in the following pages. But as a basic blueprint for leadership success, you can't do much better than this list. Every great leader I've known follows it. Work these ideas into your own repertoire and you'll be on your way to building and sustaining a collaborative, trusting, high-performance team.

Defining Leadership

I like this definition of leadership from *Leadership is an Art* by the late American businessman and writer Max De Pree: "To be a leader means, especially, having the opportunity to make a meaningful difference in the lives of those who permit leaders to lead."

There are two critical parts of this quote. The first is the idea of making "a meaningful difference." The second, and perhaps trickier part, is the idea that others *permit* leaders to lead. Let's look at each part individually.

I agree with De Pree when he suggests that being a leader entails making a *meaningful difference* in others' lives. Think about the best leader you ever had — he or she could be a manager, supervisor, sports coach, teacher, mentor, neighbor, older sibling, clergyperson, etc. I bet if you boiled down what made them so influential to *one* key characteristic, it would likely be something like "He/She made a meaningful impact on me."

That impact looks different for everyone, of course. Leader A might have helped someone get through a tough time in their life. Leader B might have shown someone how to overcome their self-imposed limitations. Leader C might have provided the support and encouragement necessary for someone to switch careers. *But at the most basic level, all great leaders make a meaningful — and often long-lasting — difference in the lives of their followers.*

Returning to De Pree's quote, the idea of "permitting" leaders to lead is not so clear-cut. Think about it: There can be no leaders without followers. Followers inform and give shape to the leader — in essence, they "permit" the leader to lead them. It's not hard to imagine what happens should that permission be revoked: Followers become bitter, resentful, and indignant, the leader/follower relationship fractures, and people start looking for the exit.

You should strive to be the kind of leader whom people *permit* to lead them — not because they fear you but because they *respect and trust* you.

At its core, this book is about how to become that type of leader. I encourage you to read it carefully, absorb its lessons, and share it with anyone whom you think will benefit. We'll start our journey by examining the CHORDS Model™, which consists of six essential "notes" all high-performing leaders, teams, and organizations play.

Now It's Your Turn: Which of the ideas presented so far are resonating most? Why?

The CHORDS Model™

Several years ago, when the idea for my company Right Chord Leadership was born, I recall searching for a single metaphor or analogy that captured the basic tenets of my approach to leadership and team development. As a professional musician since my teenage years, I landed on the idea of the *chord:* a musical term that designates a collection of notes played at the same time. If I play a chord on a piano consisting of notes that happen to blend well together, you might tell me that chord sounds *pretty, lovely,* or—if you really want to impress me—*harmonious.* However, if I play a chord consisting of notes that *don't* blend well together, you might say it sounds *jarring, harsh,* or—again, if you really want to impress me—*dissonant.*

Have you ever considered that people play chords, too? Not literally, of course, but figuratively. I think of the chords we play as the *energy* we send into the world every moment of every day. Put another way, the chords we play are reflections of the way we "show up" at work specifically and in life more generally. Sometimes our chords are *out of tune,* especially if we're having a crappy day. Out-of-tune chords consisting of "sour notes" show up as annoyance, frustration, aggravation, anger, bitterness, resentment, and a lack of patience and empathy.

But sometimes our chords are, as I like to say, *in the groove* (an old-fashioned term, perhaps, but stay with me here). To be *in the groove*—a phrase believed to have its origin in 1920s jazz vernacular—means more than simply being in a good mood. What being *in the groove* means to me is *being attuned to and in alignment with* the important people, projects, and plans in your life. When your chords are *in the groove,* you radiate positivity. You're optimistic, energetic, confident, and generous—the *opposite* of how you feel when playing dissonant chords.

The chords leaders play are *especially* critical. Leaders who consistently "strike the right chord" typically experience success. Such leaders are trusted, respected, and adept at inspiring others to do great work. However, leaders who habitually play "sour notes" erode trust and morale, foster fear and anxiety, and drive people out of the organization.

Below are two lists showing key differences between these two types of leaders:

Qualities of leaders who "strike the right chord"	Qualities of leaders who habitually play "sour notes"
Trustworthy	Unreliable
Effective communicator	Poor communicator
Accountable	Unaccountable
Focuses on the big picture and long-term goals as well as short-term objectives	Reactive, short-sighted, focuses solely on short-term objectives
Creates psychological safety	Punishes others for mistakes
Motivates	Demotivates
Self-aware	Oblivious
Stays calm under pressure	Impulsive and erratic under pressure
Humble	Arrogant
Open-minded	Closed-minded
Ethical	Unethical
Honest	Dishonest
Good mediator	Poor mediator
Makes others feel good about themselves	Makes others feel bad about themselves
Respectful	Disrespectful
Uses persuasive messaging to influence	Uses threats and fear to influence
Empathic	Insensitive
Passionate	Aloof
Focused on others' success	Focused on own success
Consistent	Inconsistent

Figure 1

I conceived the CHORDS Model to represent the key factors that distinguish great leaders and teams from average or poor ones. The CHORDS Model is the heart and soul of Right Chord Leadership. The idea is that great leaders and teams play all six notes of the Model. Above-average leaders and teams may play five, while average leaders and teams may only play four. Leaders and teams that routinely play three or fewer notes of the CHORDS Model will almost certainly experience toxic behavior and struggle mightily as a result.

CHORDS Model™

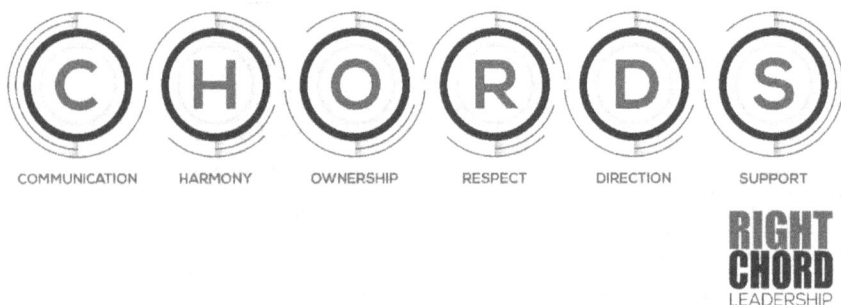

COMMUNICATION　　HARMONY　　OWNERSHIP　　RESPECT　　DIRECTION　　SUPPORT

RIGHT CHORD LEADERSHIP

Figure 2: The CHORDS Model

I'll briefly define each note here, then discuss them in more detail in future chapters.

Note 1: Communication

Leaders and team members whose messages are clear, concise, and memorable cut through the "noise" and galvanize action while reducing mistakes.

Note 2: Harmony

When leaders and team members are in sync, trust and morale flourish, collaboration increases, smart decisions are made, and problems get solved quickly.

Note 3: Ownership

When leaders and team members are accountable, they're attentive to detail, exude pride in their work, and go the extra mile for the customer and each other.

Note 4: Respect

Treating others with dignity, valuing their opinions, and validating their feelings are hallmarks of successful leaders, trusted team members, and world-class organizations.

Note 5: Direction

A bold and compelling organizational vision defines an optimal future state, serving as a vivid "North Star" that focuses, energizes, and unifies people.

Note 6: Support

Coaching, constructive feedback, and encouragement ignite a "growth mindset," motivating people to continually improve and seek new challenges.

Now It's Your Turn: What thoughts/ideas does the CHORDS Model surface for you? What relevance does the Model have to your work role?

You've read the chapter—now get the tool! Take your understanding to the next level by downloading the CHORDS Model Self-Assessment at

rightchordleadership.com/book-resources/

Emotional Intelligence (EQ)

Before we take a deeper dive into the six notes of the CHORDS Model, I want to share a few thoughts on emotional intelligence, or EQ. Just as you can't play a musical chord without a musical instrument, you can't successfully play the six notes of the CHORDS Model without a foundation of emotional intelligence. *Emotional intelligence is the label for a set of competencies that I believe form the underpinnings of success not only at work but in life.* So, while EQ itself is not a note in the CHORDS Model, it is essential for playing any of the six notes well.

A Brief History of EQ

For many years, intelligence was typically associated with one's *intelligence quotient*, better known as IQ. You've no doubt heard of IQ. Without getting too technical, IQ is a numerical score derived from a set of tests designed to measure human intelligence. An individual would complete an IQ test and receive a number. On many commonly used tests, a score of 100 is considered average, with nearly 70 percent of people falling between 85 and 115 and 95 percent of people falling between 70 and 130. The competencies assessed on an IQ test, such as reasoning, problem-solving, etc., make up what psychologists call our *cognitive* intelligence. Obviously, cognitive skills are necessary to function effectively as a leader. Your cognitive skills very likely helped you land your leadership role in the first place.

Several decades ago, however, a different way of thinking about intelligence began to emerge. This new conception of intelligence had nothing to do with traditional measures of brainpower such as getting good grades in school. Rather, *this* type of intelligence—known as *emotional* intelligence—referred to our capacity for recognizing our own feelings and those of others, for motivating ourselves, and for managing emotions well in ourselves and in our relationships (an excellent in-depth discussion of this topic can be found in *Working with Emotional Intelligence* by Daniel Goleman). This may all sound easy, but it's actually quite challenging, especially given the incredibly fast-paced, stressful world we live in. However, if your goal is to be the best leader you can be, the tools of emotional intelligence *must* be in your toolkit.

It should be noted that as a scientifically valid construct, emotional intelligence is not without its critics. However, despite criticism—and in some cases, skepticism—from the scientific community, EQ remains as popular as ever. I believe the reason for this is simple: the idea that *emotions* can foster or hinder our success makes intuitive sense. When we (or others) exhibit emotional intelligence, *good* outcomes typically result. The reverse is also true: When we (or others) *fail* to exhibit emotional intelligence, *poor* outcomes typically result. There are exceptions, of course, but for our purposes a scientifically rigorous defense of EQ's merits is unnecessary.

It's useful to think of EQ as having four dimensions:

- *Self-awareness*—recognizing your emotions from moment to moment;
- *Self-management* (also referred to as self-regulation)—controlling your emotions, especially under stress;

- *Social awareness* — acknowledging the validity of others' perspectives and exhibiting empathy; and
- *Relationship management* — getting the best out of others, having a positive influence, and building strong relationships.

If this feels like a lot of information, don't get discouraged. It sounds more difficult than it really is. Let's continue our discussion with an overview of the foundational pillar of emotional intelligence, self-awareness.

Self-Awareness

Does it occasionally feel like you're "on the go" from the moment you open your eyes in the morning? Making plans, scheduling meetings, returning emails and calls, running errands, paying bills, keeping up with the news, connecting with family and friends — we all have dozens of obligations and commitments, both large and small, that demand our attention *every day.*

Is it any wonder that we rarely (if ever) pause to take stock of our emotional state?

Think about it: When was the last time you stopped what you were doing and asked yourself, "How am I feeling *right now?*" If you don't remember, you're not alone. Most of us can't. While this may not seem important, failing to tune in to your emotions throughout the day can be problematic. That's because common, and relatively mild, emotions such as frustration and disappointment, if left to simmer for an extended period like an unattended pot of soup, can evolve into far more intense emotions with little, if any, warning. Like that pot of soup, these emotions can boil over and leave a huge mess behind.

The tendency for unaddressed emotions to escalate is one of the reasons that developing a high degree of self-awareness is important. *Self-awareness enables us to recognize our emotional states from moment to moment and the impact they're having on ourselves and those around us.* Self-awareness brings attention to what we're feeling *in that moment*, and when we're aware of what we're feeling, we can *choose* what actions to subsequently take. If we notice we're *in the groove*, fantastic! We might choose to engage in an activity that takes advantage of that positive energy, such as taking a walk, finishing chores, or calling Mom. However, if we notice we're playing some *sour notes*, we might choose to alleviate that negative energy by exercising, listening to music, or calling a friend. Of course, the actions you take are up to you. The point is, without self-awareness, our emotions (particularly the negative ones) can easily gain control and lead us down a path that may not be helpful. In other words, without self-awareness we *become more vulnerable to emotional outbursts and irrational decisions with often unwelcome consequences.*

If you see the value of self-awareness, you may be wondering how one can "plug" into their emotions from moment to moment. As I suggested earlier, our days are full of distractions that can prevent us from connecting (even briefly) to our emotions. It takes discipline and effort to increase your self-awareness, but it is possible. Doing so can yield rewards that make your life and work more meaningful and fulfilling.

Here are three suggestions for increasing self-awareness:

1. Try to *notice* your feelings more frequently throughout the day. For example, when you arrive at work *but before you start your day*, take stock of your emotions. Are you energized? Melancholy? Optimistic? Glum? If you feel good and you're playing the *right chords*, go for it! But if you notice yourself feeling flat, you may need to play some different chords to get yourself into a productive emotional "space." When I'm not feeling energized, for example, I typically take a brisk walk while listening to some upbeat music (I prefer Bob Marley, James Brown, or Earth, Wind & Fire to drive the blues away). Rearranging my emotional space in this manner — even for a few minutes — enables me to attack my to-do list refreshed and revitalized when I return.

2. It can be helpful to *name* whatever you're feeling, especially when you are feeling out of sorts. Doing so brings your emotions into your consciousness, putting them on your "radar," so to speak. Otherwise, they can toss us around like a piece of driftwood bobbing in rough surf. For example, if you're about to enter a meeting with your boss, you might say to yourself, "I'm noticing that I'm anxious." Similarly, if you receive an email from a colleague that triggers a defensive response, you might think, "I'm noticing that I'm annoyed." Psychologists suggest that naming your emotions this way can help you better connect to them and, subsequently, *manage* them. This does not mean, however, that you should roam the hallways of your workplace

proclaiming how much Sheila in Accounting pisses you off. It's important to remember that naming emotions is an *internal* process; you bring awareness to your emotional state through an inner monologue you have *with yourself.*

3. Finally, it's imperative to accept your feelings without judgment. Human beings are judgmental creatures, constantly assessing the value and/or worth of people, places, and things (including ourselves) and often doing so inaccurately. Try to dial down your "voice of judgment" and simply *observe* and *accept* your feelings as they emerge. Don't criticize or evaluate them. Recognize that you're not a bad person for feeling angry or melancholy. You're simply human. As the poet Henry Wadsworth Longfellow wrote, "Into each life some rain must fall." Keep your composure and *choose* to play different chords, if necessary. Emotions are neither good nor bad; it's how we *manage* them that makes the difference. We'll discuss that part next.

Here are some questions to help you increase your self-awareness. Take a few minutes now to think through them:

- How "plugged in" are you to your emotions from moment to moment? Do you ever stop to take stock of your emotional state throughout the day?
- What situations make you feel afraid? Sad? Anxious? Angry? Irritated? Is it long lines? Heavy traffic? Rude people? How might you better prepare for those situations so that you play the *right chords* next time?

- Do you find that strong emotions can "sneak up" on you during periods of stress? How might you become more aware of them *before* they burst out and potentially cause damage?

Another Facet of Self-Awareness

There is another dimension of self-awareness I'd like to explore because it, too, is critical to your success. This aspect of self-awareness is less about identifying emotions *in the moment* and more about gaining a better understanding of *who you are*. If recognizing your emotions from moment to moment is the "heads" side of the self-awareness coin, gaining a deeper understanding of what makes you tick is the "tails" side.

"You blows who you is" — a quote attributed to legendary jazz trumpeter Louis Armstrong (of "What a Wonderful World" fame) — speaks to this quality of self-awareness. What Louis meant was that everything that makes you uniquely *you* — your dreams, struggles, triumphs, failures, aspirations, experiences, disappointments — comes pouring out of your instrument when you play. This is particularly true of jazz musicians like Armstrong, whose improvised solos reflect a lifetime of rich and varied emotions from jubilation to bitter heartbreak. This notion that "you blows who you is" is one of the qualities I find most fascinating and endearing about jazz.

Armstrong's quote perfectly describes the idea of knowing yourself at a profoundly deep level. Just as his incredible story came spilling out of his trumpet whenever he placed it to his lips, our life experience also shows up in the chords we play each day. While it's important for all of us to be aware of those chords, it's especially so for leaders *because their actions and behaviors impact so many others.*

Here are a few questions to help you better understand, in Armstrong's words, "who you is." Take some time to reflect on them:

1. What are my core values, and do my actions align with them?
2. What are my key strengths and weaknesses?
3. How do I handle stress and challenging situations?
4. Am I satisfied with my current relationships, both personal and professional?
5. What are my long-term goals, and what steps am I taking to achieve them?
6. How do I react to criticism, and am I open to constructive feedback?
7. What activities or hobbies bring me joy and fulfillment?
8. What are my automatic thoughts in challenging situations, and do they contribute positively or negatively to my well-being?
9. How do I prioritize my time, and does it align with my values and goals?
10. What patterns do I notice in my emotions and behaviors?

Interlude: A "Music Lesson" in Self-Awareness

What do Bruce Springsteen and self-awareness have in common? A lot, it turns out. In an article on Forbes.com titled

"The Boss Gives A Leadership Lesson In Self-Awareness," author John Baldoni cites a Springsteen interview in which he discusses his then-new autobiography.

Musing on his early days as a songwriter, Springsteen recalls thinking: "If I'm going to project an individuality, it's going to have to be in my writing. So I wrote songs that were very lyrically alive and lyrically dense and they were unique. But it really came out of a motivation to where I understood I was going to have to make my mark that way."

Springsteen's story isn't exceptional. Artists of all kinds experience similar moments of self-awareness, particularly in their formative years as they are honing their craft. Unfortunately, life in the 21st century rarely affords us adequate time to cultivate that deep understanding. When we're running from meeting to meeting, striving to meet deadlines, and tethered 24/7 to our devices, finding moments of introspection to develop self-awareness can be nearly impossible.

On an informal questionnaire I use in my EQ workshops, for example, the item "I take time every day for quiet reflection" is virtually always scored lowest. I'm reminded of a senior leader at a former employer of mine who discouraged employees from reading the company newsletter during work hours. Her claim? Doing so reduced productivity. In such an environment, who would dare take time for self-reflection?

And yet, a lack of self-awareness can be enormously damaging. Here's what I suggest at a minimum: Ask yourself the following question several times a day. Doing so will zap you into the present, reconnect you to your emotional core, and give you an opportunity to change course if necessary:

What chords am I playing right now?

Remember: We play chords every minute of every day, and we can learn to regulate them accordingly.

Once you've considered the chords you're playing, take a moment to ask yourself a second question: How are they affecting me? Are they helping or hindering my effectiveness? Do I need to play some different chords to get different results? It's a quick, powerful process for amplifying your self-awareness and getting yourself playing "in tune."

Another example of self-awareness comes from Flea (real name Michael Balzary), bassist for the Red Hot Chili Peppers. Whenever I need inspiration, uplift, or just a few minutes of joy, I listen to music. But whenever I need to be reminded of what passion, commitment, and humanity look like, I turn to YouTube and watch his 2012 Rock & Roll Hall of Fame induction speech. I've watched it dozens of times and it never fails to touch me in a profoundly personal and moving way. Here is a portion of that powerful speech:

> I love music so much and all the great rockers that have come before us. It means everything in the world to me to honor that tradition. . . . Every night before we go on stage, I get on my knees and . . . pray to uplift the people that have come to see us play. . . . More than anything, the burning, intense desire that is inside of me to play music that has not diminished in the slightest, that has only deepened as time has gone on, is when we're hitting it, when we are really inside the groove, when we're on, I'm lost, man. And in that moment, I am truly free of everything, I am truly one with everything.

In less than four minutes, Flea exhibits a full range of emotion that not only resonates with me as a fellow musician but as a fellow human being. As a YouTube viewer beautifully describes it, "His heart is *completely on* during that speech."

Although we could forgive him for being self-indulgent and prideful at that moment of triumph, Flea opts instead for humility, gratitude, and appreciation. It's a remarkable moment and truly a lesson for all of us in a world consumed by suspicion, ego, and arrogance. It's a level of self-awareness — expressed with profound modesty and vulnerability — that few ever reach.

What can you partake in today that will turn *your* heart completely on?

> *Now It's Your Turn: Which of the ideas presented so far are reso-nating most? Why? What are you considering doing differently?*

Self-Management

The second dimension of emotional intelligence is *self-management* (also referred to as self-regulation). A part of the brain called the *amygdala* plays a key role here. Let me say emphatically that I am not a neuroscientist, but my under-standing is that the amygdala is largely responsible for the perception of emotions and the controlling of aggression. It's also where memories of events — and the emotions we experi-enced *during* those events — are stored.

While actual neuroscientists may take issue with the particulars of the following discussion, I feel it's in our best interest to keep things simple here. So let's begin by crediting the amygdala for the fact that humans feel *before* we think. For example, have you ever:

- Recoiled from a snake before realizing it was merely a reptilian-looking twig?
- Crossed a street at night after sensing someone walking a few steps behind you?
- Left a social gathering early because something just didn't feel right?

If you answered "yes" to any of those questions, congratulations! You are the proud owner of a fully functioning amygdala! The amygdala acts as a kind of "smoke alarm," warning us when it perceives danger (or what *could* be danger). We can then (hopefully) avoid the threat without first having to *think* about it, an advantage which can literally save our lives (or at least protect us from harm).

Such an alarm was crucial to our ancestors' survival hundreds of thousands of years ago when our prehistoric brothers and sisters faced existential threats every day. Imagine for a moment that you're out on a hunt 250,000 years ago with your trusty spear and a few of your closest buddies. Suddenly, a growling, salivating saber-toothed tiger appears. Your amygdala immediately registers that a predator is sizing you up to be a hot lunch, leading to the release of chemicals in your body that ready you for what has long been called "fight or flight":

- You hurl your spear at the predator and hope you don't miss (fight) or

- You dash up the nearest tree and shout "Nah nah nah nah nah!" at the frustrated kitty below (flight).

Either choice is clearly preferable to standing there and weighing your options. Thanks to your quick-thinking — or, more accurately, *quick-feeling* – amygdala, you survive the perilous encounter and can now pass your genes along to the next generation. Meanwhile, the big cat slinks off into the brush to nurse his shattered pride.

Fortunately, most of you reading this book no longer face daily battles for physical survival. Yet the amygdala is still very much a part of our circuitry, continuously warning of real or perceived danger in our immediate environment.

The amygdala is a handy thing to own when facing a snarling dog, oncoming train, or other physical threat, as it will help get us out of the situation (hopefully) alive and intact. The problem with the amygdala is that it doesn't distinguish well between threats to our *physical* well-being and threats to our *emotional* well-being. It just sounds the alarm regardless, *before* we've had a chance to think rationally about the severity of the threat or the consequences of our actions. That's why we often overreact to events and only later recognize our reaction was . . . well, not ideal. Let's look at a few examples.

Imagine you're behind on an important project. You're stressed and up against a tight deadline. At the peak of your irritation, you receive an email from a colleague reminding you about a meeting that afternoon. Annoyed, you respond, "I know about the meeting. I don't need the constant reminders, thanks." It takes a few minutes after pressing "Send" to realize that maybe that wasn't the best possible response. *But in that moment, your amygdala "hijacked" your thinking brain, causing you to react impulsively.* Consequently, you may have some cleaning up to do with your coworker.

Here's another example. Picture yourself at a staff meeting when your boss shares some disappointing sales numbers. She tells you and your teammates that you're going to have to work harder in the future or there could be a reduction in head count. Agitated by this news, you blurt out, "This is ridiculous! I'm already at capacity. Do you want me to sleep here too and work nights?" Your boss glares at you. You immediately think, "Maybe there was a better way to handle my frustration." Once again, your amygdala sensed a threat to your well-being—a potent brew of disrespect, potential additional work hours, and even termination—and led you down an unfortunate path of action.

Despite these examples, the fact that we feel *before* we think isn't a bad thing. Our amygdalae (plural of amygdala) saved our ancestors from plenty of dangerous situations back in the day and continue to do so in modern times. However, it should be clear by now that *this same circuitry* can lead us 21st-century humans to behave in ways that may not be ideal. In times of extreme stress, amygdala hijacks can result in irreparable damage to relationships as well as physical harm to ourselves and others.

To avoid amygdala hijacks, you need a way to prevent your amygdala from firing at inopportune times and help you avoid impulsive reactions to the kinds of stressors we face every day. The best advice I can give in these instances is to use the *pause button.*

Scientists have discovered that our "emotional" brain responds in mere milliseconds versus our slower "thinking" brain when it perceives a threat. Such speed is ideal for avoiding a baseball hurtling toward your head but not so much when you get cut off in traffic. Pausing before reacting — *even for a few seconds* — allows your thinking brain to "catch up" to your emotional brain. Those precious seconds give you time to consider the implications of your response and potentially choose a more constructive behavior to deal with the situation.

Revisiting our examples from earlier, a brief pause could have prevented you from dashing off that terse email to your colleague. It could also have helped you refrain from making that snarky remark to your boss. *Pausing really is your brain's best friend when it's feeling stressed.* But understand that it takes practice and discipline to pause at those critical moments when pausing would benefit you most.

Pausing can take many forms. Here are a few actions you can take when your amygdala threatens to lead you down an unhealthy, counterproductive path. Take a few moments to identify which ones you might take the next time you need to pause. Then, practice until you do them automatically:

- Take a short walk
- Take a few deep breaths
- Engage in some light stretching
- Close your eyes and focus on something pleasant
- Listen to a piece of music you enjoy
- Call a friend
- Eat a healthy snack

- Read an article, book chapter, or poem
- Work on a puzzle
- Draw a picture
- Watch a funny video
- Write in a journal
- Drink a glass of water

Here are some questions to help you increase your self-management skills. Take a few minutes now to consider them:

- Think about the last time you exhibited poor self-management. Did you lose your temper? Shut down and disengage? What happened?
- What was the outcome?
- If you had a do-over, what chords would you play differently to get different results? What role might pausing play?

Now It's Your Turn: Which of the ideas presented so far are resonating most? Why? What are you considering doing differently?

Social Awareness

Think of self-awareness and self-management as tools to help you get your own house "in order" before you can successfully enter *other* people's houses. Because dealing with other people is what we're going to cover next.

The third dimension of emotional intelligence is *social awareness*. Increased social awareness begins with the recognition that no matter how hard we try, we will never see things in exactly the same way. All of us have different backgrounds, values, beliefs, experiences, and opinions that influence the way we look at the world.

There's a cartoon I like that demonstrates this idea humorously. Two characters face each other in an apparent war of wills. The character on the left shouts "6!" while the character on the right shouts "9!" At their feet is a number that is clearly a "6" from the point of view of the character on the left and clearly a "9" from the point of view of the character on the right. How many disagreements, conflicts, and arguments start precisely because of this kind of difference in perspective?

In another clever cartoon, this one by Wiley Miller, a bedraggled man standing on a tiny island in the middle of the ocean spies a man on a raft approaching. "Yay! I'm saved!" he shouts excitedly. Meanwhile, the bedraggled man on the raft also exclaims, "Yay! I'm saved!" The cartoon's caption reads: "The bittersweet meeting of perception and reality." Brilliant!

Certainly, our different perspectives can be beneficial, even exhilarating. For example, a work team comprised of individuals with different points of view will likely yield better ideas and solve problems more effectively than one composed of like-minded individuals. In *that* situation, multiple perspectives can help the team see possibilities and opportunities that might otherwise remain hidden.

However, different perspectives can also lead to conflict. If I'm stuck in *my* way of thinking and you're stuck in *your* way of thinking, we can easily get bogged down in a counterproductive dispute that ultimately erodes our relationship. I've seen this a lot with different generations in the workplace.

Baby boomers, for example, have different views on what constitutes hard work than Gen Z. Neither view is necessarily right or wrong—they're just *different*.

That's where social awareness, or empathy, comes in. According to the Merriam-Webster dictionary, empathy is "the action of understanding, being aware of, being sensitive to, and vicariously experiencing the feelings, thoughts, and experience of another." Empathy is a key element of emotional intelligence because it helps us understand what others are feeling and experiencing *as if we were feeling and experiencing the same things.*

When we exhibit empathy, we strive to validate the other person's perspective *even if we don't agree with it.* We try to see the situation, problem, or issue through their eyes. This can be exceedingly difficult if we're entrenched in our own point of view. Imagine two male rams on a mountainside furiously mashing their skulls together as they fight over a female. When we go back and forth trying to convince the other person we're *right* and they're *wrong*, we're not so different from those rams. We end up with excruciating headaches and little else.

But exhibiting social awareness is more than simply remaining receptive to another's opinion; it can entail being receptive to another's *entire reality*. In a workshop I once attended, we engaged in an exercise where one partner pretended to be from the 1600s while the other partner attempted to describe the concept of email. The partner from the 1600s was instructed to question any word, idea, or concept that didn't align with their centuries-old paradigm (a fancy word for "worldview" or "mental model").

Consider what this activity required of Partner #2. He or she couldn't use any of the terms we might use today when describing email: computer, electricity, keyboard, internet, inbox, etc. The exercise forced Partner #2 to adopt the *perspective* of Partner #1 and communicate in a way that he or she would understand.

That's social awareness, i.e., empathy, in action. There are several sayings in English that get to the heart of this idea. Perhaps the most well-known is "put yourself in the other's shoes." We temporarily put aside our own "autobiography" and open ourselves up to the other's, conceding that despite our differences neither of us is necessarily right or wrong.

How, then, can we loosen our grip on our *own* assumptions and judgments and remain receptive to the perspectives of others even when—or *especially* when—we don't agree with them? I believe the answer is to become *better listeners*.

Yes, it's both that simple and that difficult.

When I first got interested in jazz as a teenager, I quickly learned how important *listening* is to playing that type of music. I realized I'd never be a good jazz musician if all I cared about was what I wanted to play, regardless of what was going on around me. I soon came to understand that such a self-centered approach is antithetical to the very spirit of jazz.

Imagine a jazz band performing a delicate ballad. After a gentle delivery of the opening melody, the lead sax player steps to the microphone and begins to play a brash, tasteless solo. The other musicians attempt to rein the saxophonist in, but he continues to play noisily and aggressively. Audience members seem puzzled as the soloist ignores the band's desperate efforts to restrain him. After a few awkward minutes, the tune mercifully ends. The soloist smiles broadly, pleased with his overwhelming display of ego, while the other band members roll their eyes in frustration.

In more than 40 years of listening to jazz and attending jazz concerts, I have *never* witnessed the scenario described above — or anything even close to it. That's because one of the first things jazz musicians learn is that, in jazz, there is no *I* and there is no *you*.

There is only we.

What a soloist plays *in each moment* influences what the musicians play behind him or her, and what the band plays behind the soloist *in each moment* influences what he or she plays. It is a symbiotic relationship with each player adjusting, in real time, to the offerings of their fellow bandmates. Sometimes the adjustments are barely perceptible; at other times, they're glaringly obvious. The point is, everyone in a jazz band is *always* listening. Listening is as fundamental to jazz as melody, harmony, and rhythm — the three foundational elements of music.

Wynton Marsalis once said, "As a jazz musician, you have individual power to create the sound. You also have a responsibility to function in the context of other people who have that power also." This is one of the reasons I find jazz bands such an apt metaphor for organizations. Just like jazz musicians, I believe leaders have a responsibility to ensure the "sound" they create through their words and deeds complements the "sound" of others. I'm not talking here about *literal* sound, as in the sound of our voices. I am referring instead to blending our thoughts and ideas with those of others in a way that acknowledges and honors their perspective rather than overpowers or dismisses it. In a word, I'm talking about *harmonizing* with another person whether or not we agree with them. Think of this idea as co-creating a space where various points of view, no matter how dissimilar, are validated and viewed as having merit. *This is the essence of jazz as well as social awareness.*

Too often, we remember the *first* part of Wynton's statement and forget the second. We often interrupt, talk over people, dismiss others' feelings, respond inappropriately, and refuse to apologize. When we behave this way habitually, others may come to see us as obnoxious at best, impossible to work with at worst.

As a leader, you are not much different from a jazz musician trying to blend their individual sound with the collective sound of the band. Think of your team as *your* band, with each player finding their own way in the "music" you're creating together. One of your jobs as a leader is to create a space at work where *harmony can flourish even when opinions differ.*

Here are some questions to help you increase your social awareness. Take a few minutes to think through them now:

- Do you consider yourself an empathic person? Why or why not?
- When someone disagrees with you, do you try to see the issue from their vantage point? Or do you stubbornly insist your way is right? What are the typical outcomes from both approaches?
- As a leader, do you subscribe more to a "my way or the highway" approach or a "let's see if we can land on a mutually satisfying path forward" approach? If the

former, what might you consider doing differently to be less dogmatic and more empathic?

Interlude: Remembering the Queen of Soul

Elvis. James Brown. Jimi Hendrix. Whitney Houston. Bob Marley. The Beatles. Michael Jackson. Prince. Nirvana. These are the Brightest of the Bright Lights in the history of popular music, the artists who not only created the music but changed it forever. They are the titans, the ones about whom we say, "Without them, there would be no _____" as we rattle off an arm's-length list of famous names. They are the kinds of artists Motown founder Berry Gordy meant when he stated, "Some artists come around once every 10 years, others once every 100 years. And some come around only once, ever."

Aretha Franklin was that kind of artist.

The first woman inducted into the Rock & Roll Hall of Fame and the undisputed Queen of Soul, Franklin's journey from a young girl singing gospel hymns in her father's Detroit church to beloved civil rights icon and international superstar is well known. And of course, her many recordings and live performances speak for themselves. Curiously, it wasn't any of those things that struck me the most when she passed away in 2018. Rather, it was what other luminaries said *about* her. A few examples:

"It's difficult to conceive of a world without her." — Barbra Streisand

"What a life. What a legacy! So much love, respect and gratitude." — Carole King

"She will be missed but the memory of her greatness as a musician and a fine human being will live with us forever." —Paul McCartney

"You were my inspiration, my mentor and my friend." —Mariah Carey

"Her passing is not only a tremendous personal loss for me, but for people all over the world who were touched by her incredible gift and remarkable spirit." —Berry Gordy

While none of us possesses Franklin's astounding gifts as a singer or her worldwide fame, we each have the same ability to touch others in a positive way through our own unique "sound." I encourage you to learn about her legacy and be inspired to leave a similar imprint on the world, such that others are compelled to say of you with equal parts joy and sadness: "It's difficult to conceive of a world without them."

Now It's Your Turn: Which of the ideas presented so far about social awareness are resonating most? Why? What are you considering doing differently?

Relationship Management

The fourth and final dimension of emotional intelligence is *relationship management*. Relationship management is about our ability to form and sustain healthy, mutually rewarding relationships (you probably figured that out already). We can build strong relationships in lots of ways, but in my experience, the most effective ways are by cultivating trust, helping others, and possessing a genuine desire to see other people succeed.

Trust

Let's start with the glue that holds together any high-performing team: trust. I want to tell you about a YouTube video titled "Colin Powell Speaks About Leadership and Trust" featuring the late Colin Powell, former U.S. Secretary of State and the first African American Secretary of State in U.S. history. (As of this book's publishing, the video can be found at a YT channel called Storyful News and Weather — search for it and you should find it.) Powell is recorded in 2011 speaking before a live audience. An audience member asks how he would define the key characteristics of effective leadership that, in her words, "allow you to go and be an advocate for good." Without hesitation, Powell replies, "Trust."

I've included the rest of his response here verbatim (with some parts edited for the sake of brevity) because I believe every leader should be familiar with his main points:

> The longer I have been in public service and the more people have asked me about leadership over the years — leadership ultimately comes down to creating conditions of trust within an organization. Good leaders are people who are trusted by followers. Leaders take organizations past the level that the science and management says is possible.

One of my sergeants back in the Infantry School at Fort Benning almost 50 years ago . . . said to me, "Lieutenant, you'll know you're a good leader when people follow you if only out of curiosity."

What he was saying . . . is they trust you and you have built up that trust. How did you do it? Clear mission and selfless service. People look to you and they trust you because you're serving selflessly as the leader — not self-serving, *selflessly.* . . .

You prepare the followers, you train them, you give them what they need to get the job done — don't give them a job if you're not going to give them the resources — and that you're prepared to take the risks with them. . . .

They'll follow you into the darkest night, down the deepest valley, up the highest hill if they trust you.

So, the essence of leadership is about doing all that the science and management says you can with resources but then taking that extra step and giving it that *spark.* And that spark comes from getting people to trust you so that they will follow you if only out of curiosity.

Think about what Powell is suggesting here. Why might someone choose to follow *you* if only out of curiosity?

Because they believe in your leadership vision.

Because they respect you.

Because they know you have their back.

Because you provide the tools and support for them to be successful.

Because you're dependable.

Because you're honest.

Because they know that wherever you take them, it's going to be in the best interest of the team and the organization.

In short, because they trust you.

I want you to put this book down for a moment and find a new, clean sheet of paper.

Now, take that piece of paper and crumple it into a ball.

Next, unfold it and attempt to remove all the creases and wrinkles using any method you wish. *Your goal here is to return that sheet of paper to its previous pristine, unblemished state.*

Go ahead, I'll wait.

I'm willing to bet that no matter how strenuously you tried to smooth it out, removing all its imperfections proved hopeless. Was I right? In my 25 years as a trainer, I've not had one participant who could return the paper to its previously flawless state.

Trust is like that piece of paper: Once it's damaged, it's practically impossible to make perfect again. Depending on the severity of the damage, the people you've hurt will always range from somewhat cautious around you to extremely suspicious.

Another familiar expression comes to mind here: Trust takes years to build and seconds to destroy.

As a leader, you need to remember this. *Trust is a fragile thing.*

Like that piece of paper.

Treat it as such.

Helping Others

Another aspect of relationship management is helping others. This probably seems obvious. But these days—with everybody stretched, resources often in short supply, and stress levels elevated—it's easy to find ourselves focused solely on our own needs while leaving others to fend for themselves.

That may be understandable, but it's not good leadership.

Remember what General Powell said about serving selflessly? He may have been referring to a leadership approach known as *servant leadership*. The term was coined by Robert K. Greenleaf in *The Servant as Leader*, an essay first published in 1970. As the name suggests, servant leadership is about leading *in the service of others*. That means your focus as a leader is not on accumulating power or material possessions but rather on the *growth and well-being of those you serve*. Servant leaders set people up to succeed and become servant leaders themselves.

Not every leader strives to be a servant leader, of course. In fact, a depressingly high number of leaders conduct themselves in ways that run directly counter to the very notion of servant leadership. You don't need to look far to spot them. Our educational, financial, government, cultural, healthcare, technology, media, military, and, ironically, nonprofit institutions are rife with them. Such leaders place themselves before everyone else. They see the role of leader primarily as a means to grab as much power, collect as much wealth, and subjugate as many people as possible. Unfortunately, they do occasionally succeed despite their wretched behavior.

Hey, nobody ever said life was fair.

You may be thinking servant leadership sounds interesting but impractical: "It's intriguing, but I don't see it working. If you don't show 'em who's boss, people will run all over you."

If you have misgivings about servant leadership, I understand. It may not be the approach you've seen some of your leaders take (and haven't *they* been successful?). Or perhaps the idea of sharing power, putting the needs of others first, and helping people develop and perform as well as possible doesn't fit *your* conception of what leadership is all about. After all, servant leadership is rarely celebrated on reality shows or in the media.

You're certainly entitled to adopt an approach to leadership that works for you. But I know this: *servant leadership works.*

How do I know? Because nearly *everyone* wants to work for a leader who puts their people before him- or herself.

An illustrative example of servant leadership involves David Packard of Hewlett-Packard fame. The story is told of a barbecue that Packard once hosted at his ranch near San Jose, California. After the guests left, Packard assisted in putting the folding chairs away until they'd all been properly stored. "Dave came over and took three chairs in one hand and three in another hand, and worked right alongside me until the job was done," recalled one attendee. "With all his fame and wealth and fortune and respect, here he is putting the chairs away. He leads by example." (Source: "The passing of a legend," paloaltoonline.com, Publication Date: Friday, March 29, 1996).

If you want to improve your relationship management skills, start with these six recommendations:

1. **Be genuinely interested in other people.** There is a saying that goes: "There are two kinds of people. The first kind walks into a room full of people and says 'Here I am.' The second kind walks into the same room and says, 'There you are.'" Individuals with strong relationship management skills focus on other people rather than themselves.

2. **Give others your undivided attention.** We covered this idea earlier when we discussed social awareness, but it bears mentioning again here. When you are engaged with another person in a conversation, do everything you can to stay focused and present. Don't allow yourself to become distracted by what's going on around you. Don't interrupt or finish their sentences, either. Your full attention is a gift the other person will surely appreciate.

3. **Be on time for appointments.** Nothing says "I don't value your time" like routine tardiness. I recently had lunch with a colleague named Curt who served in the military. He called me to say he was running about five minutes behind. I laughed and told him not to worry about it, that five minutes was nothing. He replied, "Where I come from, not arriving five minutes *early* is considered late." Take Curt's advice: Plan to arrive five to ten minutes early for any appointment so you can get settled and be completely ready at the

scheduled time. And if you are running late, be sure to give the other person a heads-up.

4. **Be reliable 100 percent of the time.** You can't be reliable *some* of the time—either you're a reliable person or you're not. Say what you're going to do and then do it. If a problem arises, don't wait to let the other person know. And if it's *your* fault, don't blame others. Take responsibility for the problem and resolve to fix it.

5. **Ask others how you can help.** People with strong relationship management skills primarily see themselves as being in service to others. Share your time, wisdom, and resources with those who could benefit. Your generosity will come back to you.

6. **Be kind and courteous.** Treat others the way you would want to be treated. A little kindness and courtesy can be remarkably effective at strengthening relationships and are at the heart of good relationship management.

Interlude: All About That Bass

Unless you're a serious jazz head, you probably haven't heard of the late bassist Gary Peacock. But Peacock's pedigree is impressive: He played with such jazz legends as Bill Evans, Miles Davis, Keith Jarrett, Jack DeJohnette, and a host of others. I recently came across an article on the NPR website titled "Bassist Gary Peacock Is At The Soloist's Service." Naturally, I was intrigued!

For me, the last paragraph was the most eye-opening part of the article:

> My whole orientation [as a bass player] was more of service, more of like wanting to contribute to the welfare of whoever's playing the solo. . . . In other words, what can I play so that this person just plays the best he's ever played?

That last sentence is crucial to understanding the jazz mindset: *What can I play so that this person just plays the best he's ever played?* One of the great rewards of listening to—and especially performing—jazz is the empathic orientation of musicians like Peacock. You can hear that high level of support (sometimes subtle but always present) baked right into the music, and the results are often stunning.

Look at how, with just a few small tweaks, Peacock's sentiment beautifully captures what I believe is the essence of leadership: *"How can I lead so that my team member performs the best he or she has ever performed?"* Since the start of my career as a consultant, I've maintained that the fundamental role of leadership is to provide the necessary support, encouragement, resources, and environment for people to do their best work. That's why I encourage leaders to take a page from Peacock's playbook and ask that question every day. The *best* leaders I know ask themselves that question continually. They don't even think about it; it's just a fundamental element of their approach to leadership.

How can you lead so that your people perform the best they've ever performed?

Strengthening Your Emotional Intelligence

There you have it—the four dimensions of emotional intelligence: self-awareness, self-management, social awareness, and relationship management. Identify which dimension presents *your* greatest opportunity for development and start small with a single behavioral change. Remember—just *thinking* about doing things differently isn't enough. *You must be willing to change your behavior if you want results!*

Focus on that one behavioral change until it becomes natural. Then, choose another and work on that. Strengthening emotional intelligence is a lifelong commitment. It takes effort and motivation, but the results will be worth it!

Of course, you will occasionally cross paths with people who aren't interested in strengthening their emotional intelligence. Many years ago, I was facilitating a workshop for a team of labor and delivery nurses at a large Philadelphia hospital. One of the senior nurses who'd worked there for decades (I'll call her Mary) shared an issue that was causing problems on the team. I listened carefully and responded, "What different chords might you play to get different results?" Mary chuckled and said, "Oh please, I've been here since the Liberty Bell cracked."

I don't recall what came next, but that line has always stayed with me. It's code for "I've been here a long time, and I'm not about to change for anything or anyone." Whenever I relate that story, it always gets a laugh. Everybody knows a Mary—someone who is unwilling to reflect on their behavior and consider changing it for the better. After all, it's easier to blame others.

A big part of being an emotionally intelligent person is learning how to work with the Marys you'll inevitably meet in your life. Although there's no simple formula for dealing with them, I find it useful to remember that *everyone you meet is carrying a burden you can't see*. For some, it may be a sick child or parent. For others, it may be financial difficulties or a rocky marriage. As a colleague of mine once humorously suggested, some may be carrying a small suitcase while others are driving a U-Haul. Still others may be piloting a FedEx plane! Whatever a person is carrying often "leaks out" in the form of difficult or seemingly irrational behavior.

Here is where a little grace and patience can help. I'm not justifying difficult behavior or suggesting it's not challenging. I'm simply reminding you what Gandhi purportedly said, "To lose patience is to lose the battle." I think this is particularly true with people who lack emotional intelligence.

A Few Words About Conscientiousness

Conscientiousness is considered a key ingredient for success. People who are *conscientious* set and keep long-range goals, make thoughtful choices, behave cautiously rather than impulsively, and take obligations to others seriously. Conscientious individuals tend to be prepared, reliable, and attentive. They attend to tasks without delay, are likely to be organized and deliberate, arrive on time, and follow rules. In short, they are typically disciplined, high-achieving, and tuned in to the needs of others.

Research shows that people who test high in conscientiousness get better grades in school, commit fewer crimes, and stay married longer. They have fewer strokes, lower blood pressure, and a lower incidence of Alzheimer's disease. Some studies even suggest that conscientiousness is the most important factor for finding and retaining employment.

When we first meet someone, there's no way to know how conscientious they are. We can only determine that by spending time with them and seeing how they behave. You can't see, hear, or feel conscientiousness itself, but you can surely observe the behavior of a conscientious person.

Take a moment to think of someone you know who is conscientious. What characteristics or qualities do they demonstrate?

On the flip side, a *less* conscientious person tends to avoid tasks that require action and/or complete tasks in a careless fashion. They prefer to live "in the moment" rather than consider the consequences of their actions. They are often inattentive and neglectful of their commitments and obligations. People who lack conscientiousness tend to be late, unable to find what they need when they need it, and prone to procrastination. These behaviors can result in confusion and resentment in others.

How can you develop conscientiousness as a leader? Start by accepting that *being conscientious is a choice,* one you either make or reject. It's what we call an "either/or" proposition — you either are or you aren't. If you want to be more conscientious, start by focusing on three things:

- **Concentrate on a specific area**. Choose one area of your life in which you want to be more thoughtful and purposeful rather than reactive or impulsive. For example, at first you might focus your efforts on being punctual, maintaining a neater desk, or responding to emails quicker. Even simple things such as returning other people's property in a timely manner, showing up for an appointment on time, or sticking to a deadline reflect conscientious behavior. Then, move on to another area and keep going until you become hard-wired for conscientiousness in all aspects of your life.

- **Take time to plan.** Conscientious people do a lot of planning, which goes a long way toward helping them get more organized and in control of their life. Setting up bill-paying schedules to avoid late fees, planning purchases rather than buying things on impulse, creating realistic daily schedules, and leaving sufficient time to complete tasks are all important aspects of being conscientious.

  Keep yourself focused by making daily plans and using reminder tools such as software or smartphones to help you stay on track (or keep it simple by using pen and paper). Setting your own schedule and then following through encourages self-discipline. But of course, you need to stick to the plans you make.

- **Stay social**. A large component of conscientiousness is being social. During the COVID-19 pandemic, when it seemed as if the whole world shut down, we had no choice but to isolate ourselves. However, we soon discovered just how detrimental isolation can be. One of the challenges with isolation is that when you keep to yourself for long periods, it's easy to slip into habits that are not conscientious. When the world finally opened up and we were free to venture outside, many of us had to "unlearn" the habits we'd developed and recall how to interact with others face-to-face. For example, my first in-person workshop following months of Zoom and Microsoft Teams meetings was shaky. It took me several hours to find my footing and feel comfortable speaking in front of an audience again. It was an important reminder that networking, staying in touch with family and friends, and grabbing the occasional coffee or lunch with a colleague is not only good for the soul but can encourage conscientious behaviors like being prompt and expressing gratitude.

Here's the bottom line: If you want to become a more conscientious leader, you need to remember that *you* are in control of your behavior. Whether you fail or succeed depends almost entirely on you ("almost" because there are often factors at play beyond our control). Once you accept that reality, start working on those dimensions of your leadership that need strengthening until you reach the point where you're experiencing improved results. Then, select another facet of your leadership and work on *that* one. Continual learning is a hallmark of successful people in every walk of life.

Now that you have a firm grasp of what emotional intelligence is and why it matters, let's begin our exploration of the individual notes of the CHORDS Model. We'll begin with Note #1: Communication.

Note 1: Communication

Leaders whose messages are clear, concise, and memorable cut through the "noise" and galvanize action.

One of my favorite quotes is credited to the great Irish playwright George Bernard Shaw: "The single biggest problem in communication is the illusion that it has taken place." If you have ever conveyed a message that was misunderstood, misinterpreted, or misconstrued by the other party, you know *exactly* what Mr. Shaw is talking about. Due to the different ways people process information—not to mention the idiosyncratic nature of language itself—even messages we think are crystal-clear can get twisted. Sometimes badly so.

A memorable example of a receiver misinterpreting a simple message occurred many years ago when I worked at QVC, the televised home shopping channel. I'd left a voicemail after work for a colleague, and although I don't recall it exactly, the message went something like this: "Hi_____, it's Mike. I'm driving home and thinking about the XYZ project, which I think is pretty pathetic. Let's connect tomorrow when you have some time."

The next day, my colleague appeared in my cubicle looking annoyed. "I got your message," she said. "What makes you think the project is pathetic?"

At first, I couldn't imagine what she was talking about. Then, it dawned on me. I explained that it wasn't the *project* I thought was pathetic but rather the fact that I was *thinking about it* on my drive home. In that moment, it occurred to me how easily even seemingly simple messages can get warped.

The ability to communicate clearly is one of the most important skills a leader can possess. Whether you're communicating with a boss, colleague, client, or vendor, the quality of your communication has a tremendous impact on your success. Poor communication skills will almost certainly negatively affect the way people view you. You may be perceived as unintelligent at best, dishonest or unethical at worst. But if you speak and write clearly and confidently, you will leave a positive impression on those who interact with you. Improving your communication skills is something you can—and should—work on every day. Let's start by focusing on an aspect of language that can compromise the effectiveness of your communication through no fault of your own.

In my workshops on communication, participants engage in an exercise called "Draw A Bug." I ask for a volunteer to come to the front of the room and describe an illustration of a cartoon ladybug displayed on my computer screen (the other participants can't see the picture). I instruct the participants to draw what the volunteer describes *as accurately as possible*. After three minutes, the volunteer is usually out of ideas, and we give him or her a round of applause.

Next, I reveal the ladybug while the participants reveal their *own* drawings to each other. While some drawings resemble the volunteer's more than others, *not one is ever an exact duplicate*. In fact, most of the participants' drawings barely resemble the original ladybug (thus allowing me to engage in some gentle ribbing about their artistic capabilities).

Next, I ask the participants what happened: Why don't their bugs resemble the volunteer's drawing with greater precision? Some claim the differences are simply a matter of artistic talent. While true to a point, I suggest there is something else more profound at work: The primary reason why everyone's artwork is different has more to do with the way we *perceive information* than our drawing skills.

I've conducted this exercise dozens of times and noticed that when volunteers describe the ladybug, they invariably leave out vital details that would have increased the accuracy of the participants' drawings. For example, volunteers typically say "The ladybug has two wings" or "The ladybug has six legs" yet fail to mention the *size, shape, or length* of those body parts.

Similarly, volunteers often state that the ladybug is smiling without mentioning they are viewing a *cartoon* ladybug. Without that crucial piece of information, the notion of a "smiling ladybug" is confusing at best and inconceivable at worst.

As the exercise continues, the opportunity for misinterpretation increases because even simple words such as "antenna," "eye," "body," and "feet" become fuzzy when processed through the lens of each participant's unique perspective. How long is the antenna? Is it straight or curved? What size and shape are the eyes? How long is the body? Are the feet big or small? And since when have ladybugs had feet in the first place?

Little wonder, then, that so much variation exists among the drawings when they're finally revealed. A quote attributed to the writer Anaïs Nin sums up this phenomenon perfectly: "We don't see things as they are, we see them as we are."

If you want to be an effective communicator, it's crucial to remember the key lesson of the "Draw A Bug" exercise: Although our messages may be perfectly clear *to us*, everyone interprets and processes information differently. This notion is summed up by an illustration in one of my PowerPoint decks. On the left is a straight arrow labeled "What we *think* we're giving." Next to it, an arrow resembling a hopelessly tangled knot is labeled "What they're *actually* hearing." It's a clever reminder that what we *mean* isn't what matters; it's what the other person *understands* that matters.

Clear, concise messaging is important in *every* communication context. Whether you're providing feedback, asking for a favor, or outlining a strategy, strive to minimize the chance for misinterpretation. Keep your communication free of ambiguous words and phrases that can lead to confusion.

For example, many of us use "ASAP" as a shorthand for "as soon as possible." We might tell a coworker "I'll get you that report ASAP" or "I'll be at the meeting ASAP." But what does "as soon as possible" *really* mean? In the next minute? The next hour? The next day? The next week? Without additional context, it could mean any of those things!

Instead of using ASAP, I suggest being more specific: "I'll get you that report *by 3 p.m. today*" or "I'll be at the meeting *within the next 15 minutes*." Clear, concise language reduces the possibility of misunderstandings.

The same holds true for your written communication, where abbreviations and emojis often substitute for actual words. With emails, text, and other forms of written communication, your recipient only has words on a screen. There is no accompanying body language or tone of voice that could add clarity to your message. Nor is there an opportunity to ask questions or check for understanding. It's important to be clear in all your communication *but especially in what you write.*

The Three V's of Communication

Let's broaden this discussion a bit. When it comes to the quality of your spoken messages, think of yourself as the "sender" and the other person as the "receiver." Now, consider that spoken messages are significantly more complicated than we were taught in elementary school. In fact, it could be asserted that spoken messages have at least *three dimensions* which are known collectively as the "Three V's": Visual, Vocal, and Verbal. Recognizing how the Three V's work together to either enhance or weaken your spoken communication is essential to your success as a leader.

The first V stands for Visual. This component concerns how you look. Are you well-groomed? Are you dressed appropriately? Do you appear confident and credible? The second V, which stands for Vocal, concerns the quality of your voice and includes pitch, rate or speed, clarity, volume, and tone. The third V, which stands for Verbal, concerns the words you use. Are they too basic for the receiver, too complex, or just right?

The best communicators keep *all three dimensions* in mind:

- Their dress, posture, and overall appearance lends them credibility, whether speaking to one person or a large audience.
- They don't talk in a monotone but rather make full use of their voice to add energy and variety to their speech.
- They use words their receiver(s) will clearly understand—in other words, they *calibrate* their language appropriately for their audience, avoiding language that is too difficult or too simple.

It's important to remember the Three V's no matter who you are communicating with. Let's examine each one in more depth.

The First V: Visual

Fairly or not, your physical appearance is the first thing people pay attention to. Whether you realize it or not, before you open your mouth people have begun to judge you. They are sizing you up based on the way you look, which includes your clothes, your level of hygiene and grooming, and other physical attributes.

Of course, we can never be certain what kind of shirt or belt may appeal to a stranger. Many years ago, I saw a YouTube video called "The Power of First Impressions" in which several job recruiters discuss which physical attributes they dislike in a job candidate. One recruiter, for example, admits that strong perfume or aftershave is a turnoff. Another shares that she would hesitate to employ a man with "fair eyelashes." A third admits she is "not crazy" about "gray shoes." A researcher featured in the video states that people tend to form an opinion about a person *within the first 15 seconds* of meeting them. I've also seen research suggesting that number is closer to 7 seconds!

While you can't anticipate what others may prefer when it comes to shoes, necklaces, and hair styles, the video reminds us that people start making up their minds about us quickly. In my experience, dressing neatly and professionally is a *minimal* requirement for success as a leader. You don't have to look or dress like a movie star, but at the very least, you need to avoid looking sloppy. If you're going to work, dress according to company protocol. If you're going to an interview, dress appropriately. If you're not sure what to wear, research the company culture or ask someone. Remember: How you look gives people a window into what you're about. And whether you like it or not, people will draw conclusions about you based on what they *see*.

Assuming your clothes look fine, make sure you have clean hair and well-groomed nails. Tattoos and piercings may be acceptable at your organization or they may not be. It's important that you understand company policy *before* you apply to work there. If you want to get a tattoo or piercing *after* you're hired, I suggest checking with your manager and/or HR first. Also, recognize that while some folks may be fine with body art, others will not be—and that is their prerogative. I would never tell you how to dress or adorn your own body; I'm simply encouraging you to be smart about it.

Body language, or "nonverbal cues," is another aspect of the Visual component of communication. It includes eye contact, gestures, and facial expressions. Increasing eye contact, for example, makes others feel that you are interested in what they have to say (too much, though, will come across as creepy). Gestures can complement your words, but too many will make you appear frantic or nervous.

Facial expressions convey emotions even when you're not aware of making them, so be careful. Some people have a good "poker face"—they're able to keep their face from revealing inner thoughts and feelings. Others "wear their heart on their sleeve," meaning their emotions are easy for others to perceive. No matter which describes you, be aware that we often make facial expressions without realizing it. For example, if someone we don't like comes in the room, we may roll our eyes or look as if we just bit into a lemon. We may not *realize* we're doing it, but the other person is likely to notice regardless. Keep in mind that we're communicating *all the time* through body language, even when our lips aren't moving.

In the video I referenced earlier on first impressions, we see a fascinating social experiment play out in real time. A job recruiter is instructed to turn the dial of a small machine as she interviews three job candidates—clockwise if the candidate is making a positive impression at that moment or counterclockwise if the candidate is making a negative impression at that moment. The movements of the dial are tracked on a computer screen that we, the viewer, can see, but the candidates cannot see the machine or the screen.

Within 12 seconds of the first candidate's interview, the recruiter turns the dial way up, indicating an excellent first impression. Since the candidate has spoken only five words at this point, it is reasonable to conclude that the high score primarily reflects the first V (Visual). Indeed, Candidate #1 is smartly dressed with tasteful accessories and an overall professional appearance. For the duration of the interview, her line remains well above average.

Let's now examine the second V—Vocal.

The Second V: Vocal

In addition to how they appear, good communicators are aware of the vocal quality of their speech, like their tone, pitch, rate or speed, volume, emphasis, and enunciation. The way you use your voice undoubtedly impacts the quality of your communication. For example, think of all the different ways you can say the phrase "Have you seen my wallet?" You can ask in a polite and gentle way, an irritated way, a puzzled way, or about 100 other different ways! You can ask it slowly, quickly, loudly, or softly. You can slur the words together or pronounce each one distinctly. You can speak them in a high-pitched voice or a low-pitched voice. The point is, *your voice is an amazingly versatile instrument that the best communicators use to its fullest potential.*

To improve the vocal quality of your voice, don't speak in a monotone. A flat, unwavering tone can quickly grow boring for the listener. Instead, take full advantage of the flexibility of your voice by modifying your rate, volume, and pitch. Speed up and slow down appropriately. Emphasize certain words. Speak quietly at times and more loudly at others. There is no formula for how to do this effectively; you need to be aware of what the situation calls for and adjust accordingly.

A great tip is to watch excellent speakers at their craft. There are plenty of TED talks available on YouTube, for example. Some are better than others, but you're focusing on the speaker here rather than the content. The best presenters use their voice like an instrument, taking advantage of its full potential to create drama. Take notes and then practice, practice, practice to unlock the musicality of *your* voice.

Let's return to the first impressions video. Recall the machine that tracks, in real time, the impressions each candidate makes on the recruiter. In the opening moments of the *second* candidate's interview, the line tracking the recruiter's dial movements starts slightly above average (indicating that the candidate looks fine). Soon, however, the line starts to dip. The unseen researcher, who is observing the proceedings in a back room, remarks on camera: "Listen to [the candidate's] voice—it's beginning to lack expression." The trace continues to drop as the candidate's voice adopts a bland, almost monotone quality. The recruiter is losing interest. *It's a compelling example of how the Vocal aspect of our spoken messaging can negatively impact us even if we "look the part."*

The *third* candidate's interview is the most telling. Unbeknownst to the recruiter, *this* candidate is a paid actress. Although she *looks* legit, she was instructed to appear nervous, act evasively, and not smile or look the recruiter in the eye. It doesn't help that she enters the interview room carrying shopping bags, resulting in her trace plummeting *before she speaks a single word*. Things get worse from there, and as expected, her final trace ends up well below the other two candidates. Interestingly, the video notes that *within the first five seconds* of their respective interviews, the three candidates have already been ranked in order: Candidate #1 in first place, Candidate #2 in second place, and Candidate #3 in third place. *And that order never changes.*

Think about that for a moment: Within the first five seconds of each interview, the recruiter had made her mind up about each candidate, and her initial impression never wavered. If you don't think your communication success is influenced by how you look *and* sound, I urge you to reconsider.

The Third V: Verbal

The third dimension of communication, Verbal, concerns the actual words you use (also known as *content*). Simply put, good communicators tailor their language to "fit" their audience. Are you speaking to a mechanical engineer? A poet? An architect? An attorney? It's not merely a matter of trying to sound smart; rather, it's about *communicating in a way that resonates with your intended audience* — whether it's one person or 1,000.

While the words you choose are important, there is more to the Verbal dimension of communication. How well the words you choose *go together* is also crucial. Are your thoughts clear? Do they flow smoothly from one to the other? Can the listener "paint a picture" of what you're talking about in their mind? If you've ever spoken to someone whose speech is jumbled, you know how challenging it can be just to stay engaged in the conversation.

Let's take a moment to discuss "filler" words such as "um," "uh," "right," "you know," "like," and "I mean." It's amazing how often I hear people — especially Millennials and Gen Zers — using these expressions, which both distract the receiver *and* detract from the meaning of your speech. Additionally, overusing fillers can make you seem unsure or unprepared. A few filler words here and there may not sabotage your message, but an overabundance of them will. Receivers will begin to focus on *them* rather than on your content. After a while, people will lose interest and check out.

Pop singer Ariana Grande is a notable example of a talented person with less-than-ideal communication skills. I recently watched an interview with Miss Grande on YouTube titled "Filler Words in English (from an interview with Ariana Grande)" and was both amused and shocked at the number of fillers baked into her responses. Here is an *actual transcript* of a one-minute portion of that interview:

> I feel very open and like honest and chill and like I feel like myself again you know? I feel like for a while it was like . . . not so much . . . but yeah but like now it's like it's good like my Mom cries when we Facetime because like I'm so happy and OK that's good like when you're like that good that your Mom's like "Hi sweetheart! How are you?" And I'm like "I'm good" and she's like "I can tell." I think it's like a combination of everything, I think it's like personal growth um . . . I spent a [expletive] ton of time in therapy last year um which is great like working on yourself rehearsing like dedicating yourself to your craft like just making healthy choices, you know?

My intent in sharing this is not to pick on Ms. Grande. I simply wish to point out that, while such speech may be acceptable in certain contexts, I don't associate it with successful leadership. Keep in mind that overusing filler words is a *habit*. As with any habit, replacing it with a new, more constructive behavior requires regular practice. Here are some tips my clients have found helpful:

- **Pause and breathe.** Try to catch yourself before using a filler word and pause. This brief break in your speech can give you just enough time to gather your thoughts. The best communicators pause frequently: think of pausing as the verbal equivalent of a comma.

- **Practice mindful speaking.** "Mindful" speaking means speaking with a heightened sense of awareness and intentionality. First, slow down! Communicating is not a timed sport. Speak deliberately without hurrying. This technique alone will likely reduce the number of filler words. Second, focus on the flow of your words and sentences rather than trying to fill every moment with sound.

- **Plan, prepare, and practice.** If you're speaking on a particular topic, carve out plenty of time beforehand to get familiar with your content and rehearse. Knowing your material thoroughly will help you feel more confident and in control, thereby reducing the tendency to use filler words.

- **Record yourself.** In my presentation skills workshop, I have participants record themselves on their phones and watch the videos during breaks. Participants are often mortified by the number of fillers they use, even within a short period of time. Observing where and when you tend to use fillers can raise your awareness and help you see where adjustments should be made.

- **Ask for feedback.** Ask people you trust to give you feedback on your use of fillers. For example: "I'm working on reducing the amount of filler words I use and would appreciate if you'd point them out when you hear them."

- **Stay attuned to your chords.** I've observed that people tend to use filler words when they're either overly anxious or overly relaxed. If you're someone who tends to get nervous when communicating, there are plenty of articles and videos (not to mention coaches like me) that can help you develop more confidence and composure. On the other hand, if filler words tend to sneak into your speech when you're feeling most at ease, you'll want to dial up your attentiveness to the Verbal dimension of your communication.

Now that we've discussed filler words specifically, here are a few more ways to strengthen the Verbal dimension of your communication:

- **Expand your vocabulary.** If you use only a limited number of words when you communicate, you won't be as effective as someone with a broader vocabulary. Try to learn at least one new word every day. For example, think of all the ways a person can reach their car. They can walk to the vehicle, of course, but they can also *run, march, stroll, stride, stagger, saunter,* or *amble.* Notice how those words are more interesting than "walk." They paint a more vivid picture for the listener.

- **Choose your words thoughtfully.** Conversely, using fancy vocabulary when simpler language will suffice can also compromise your communication. As I've been stressing, effective communication isn't a matter of using esoteric words to sound intelligent—*it's about using words that fit the occasion and align with your audience's needs and expectations.* For example, you may be comfortable using slang or even profanity with your friends. But if you use such language with your supervisor, you may lose your job. Be smart and remember: When it comes to playing the right chords, your words matter.

Interlude: U2 and the Power of Words

U2 guitarist the Edge (real name David Howell Evans), considered one of the most innovative guitarists of all time, once said: "Notes actually do mean something. They have power. I think of notes as being expensive. You don't just throw them around. I find the ones that do the best job and that's what I use."

What strikes me about this quote is that its inherent truth extends beyond the world of music to the world of words (and, by extension, the world of leadership). Like notes, *words* have power. They're "expensive." You don't just throw them around.

When I was a copywriter back in the '90s, I interviewed with a well-known hotshot creative director at one of Philadelphia's top advertising agencies. As he thumbed through my portfolio, his face adopted the expression of someone who'd just unknowingly taken a swig from a bottle of rancid milk.

"Your portfolio sucks," he announced matter-of-factly, tossing it disdainfully across the table.

Interview over.

More recently, a colleague advised me to substitute the phrase "My pleasure" for "No problem." At first, I didn't think such a small change would matter. Turns out I was wrong. "My pleasure" conveys that assisting others is . . . well, a pleasure; "No problem" suggests that lending a hand is typically a bother. Side note: the folks who work at Chick-fil-A routinely use "My pleasure" rather than "No problem." Obviously, it's part of their training, and I applaud them for it.

The Edge's quote also reminds me of that old cliche: *less is more*. This is as true with words as it is with music notes. There's power in brevity. Lincoln's renowned Gettysburg Address, for example, includes just 272 words and was uttered in less than three minutes. The most famous ad slogan in history, Nike's "Just do it," consists of only three words. Subway's popular slogan, "Eat fresh," has only two!

The Edge's bandmate, lead singer Bono, once said, "Music can change the world because it can change people." So can words. Use care in how you deploy them.

Executive Presence and Communication

I would be remiss if I didn't consider executive presence and its relationship to communication. Executive presence encompasses several qualities, including poise, appearance, and believability, as well as clarity of communication. People with executive presence exude confidence without ever tipping over into arrogance. They are well-spoken, self-aware, good listeners, calm under stress, and politically savvy.

You don't have to be an extrovert or gregarious to exude executive presence. You just have to inspire confidence in others that you're capable, dependable, and thoughtful.

Executive presence and communication go hand in hand because both impact the other and are central pieces of your overall "leadership brand." As I discussed earlier, when people see, hear, and interact with you, they quickly get a sense for what you're all about. In a matter of seconds, they size you up as confident or meek, articulate or tongue-tied, knowledgeable or uninformed. The longer your interaction, the greater the impression you make. If you communicate with competence, confidence, and composure, your executive presence will be strengthened as well. *In short, you'll look and sound like a leader.*

So how do you build executive presence? Let's revisit the Three V's for some ideas:

- **Exude confident body language (Visual).** Stand and sit erect. Keep your head up. Don't slouch. Walk with purpose.
- **Convey energy and enthusiasm (Visual and Vocal).** Smile. Shake hands. Move about the room with vitality. Speak with enthusiasm. Demonstrate that you're happy to be wherever you are.
- **Remain in control if things go wrong (Visual, Vocal, and Verbal).** Things don't always go as planned. When they do go awry, stay calm and composed. Consider your options rationally and make sound decisions. Don't blame others or throw a tantrum. Keep your wits about you and act and speak with conviction.
- **Make eye contact (Visual).** In the U.S., eye contact typically demonstrates interest and attentiveness. Avoid getting distracted by other activities in the room. Stay focused and be present when engaged with others.

- **Speak clearly (Vocal and Verbal)**. Don't mumble. Articulate your words with precision. Don't talk too quickly or slowly. Use an appropriate level of volume and avoid speaking in a monotone.

It's no secret that people make assumptions based on the quality of our communication. How smart are we? How dependable? How trustworthy? How credible? When the visual, vocal, and verbal aspects of your communication are in alignment, you will be an effective communicator and subsequently put a shine on your executive presence. Remember: practice, persistence, and patience are the keys to success!

Listening

Listening is an often overlooked but critical aspect of the Communication note of the CHORDS Model. In fact, you can't play that note in tune without good listening skills!

Have you ever heard the words *hearing* and *listening* used interchangeably? It's commonly done, but they aren't the same:

- *Hearing* is the ability to perceive sounds by detecting vibrations through the ear.
- *Listening* is a conscious act we do when attempting to interpret or understand a sound.

We *hear* sounds all day, but we *listen* when we pay attention and expend effort to make sense of those sounds.

Why is listening such a key leadership tool? *Because it is only through listening that we can begin to understand someone else's perspective or point of view.* Listening requires us to momentarily put aside our own point of view and open ourselves up to an alternative one. That means accepting the possibility that our perspective isn't necessarily the only one *or even the right one*, which is hard for some people. Remember the two cartoon characters fighting about whether the number between them was a 6 or a 9? I'm willing to bet neither was listening to the other.

Add in all the distractions and noise we face — emails, texts, ringing phones, meetings, interruptions, crying infants, lawn mowers, street construction, traffic, loud music — and listening becomes even *more* challenging. Yet I believe listening with intention and focus is *the most powerful skill we have* for increasing our awareness of others' needs. A wise person once observed that the word "listen" shares the same letters as the word "silent." It's a good reminder that the *less* we talk, the *more* we're likely to learn and ultimately understand about another person.

Fortunately, there's an app you can begin using right away to strengthen your listening skills. You won't find it on your smartphone, however. This app is an acronym that stands for **A**ttending, **P**robing, and **P**araphrasing. Let's look at each in turn.

Attending

Attending means giving someone your full attention. It indicates that you are present, focused, and interested in the other person (as opposed to "attending" a social function and spending the entire time on your phone). Attending encourages the other person to share freely because they know you're listening.

Have you ever been in a conversation with someone who was obviously distracted? Perhaps he or she was glancing at their watch, looking around the room, or simply staring off into space. When you observed this, did you feel as if what you were sharing wasn't important? Did you become irritated or disengage from that person altogether? I know I have on occasion.

Good listeners use their *whole body* to demonstrate interest. They maintain eye contact, nod intermittently, lean forward, and sit erect. But if it's challenging to sustain interest in person, it's even more so on the phone. Without the visual cues that would normally be available to us during an in-person exchange, we must rely on our voice to attend to the other person. This requires a great deal of discipline and self-control.

One of the most memorable examples of attending I've ever heard came from a workshop attendee. I'd asked the audience to identify the best boss they'd ever had and to explain *why* they selected that individual. This attendee described a manager who would stop what she was doing and face you whenever you popped into her office. "She believed that a live human being deserved her attention more than whatever else she was doing," the attendee said. "I haven't reported to her in over 20 years, but I still remember that."

Whenever I tell that story today, people respond similarly: "I wish *my* boss did that." When you stay focused on the other person, you are literally giving them the *gift* of your attention.

Probing

Probing (i.e., asking questions) is another important aspect of intentional listening. Asking questions not only shows you care about the other person but can also uncover valuable information. As legendary football coach Lou Holtz purportedly said, "I never learn anything talking. I only learn things when I ask questions."

There are different types of questions, but the important thing is to ask them with sincerity and genuine curiosity. Here are a few examples:

- Can you tell me more?
- Are you OK?
- How did that happen?
- What caused that?
- What did you do?
- What did you *want* to do?
- How did you feel about that?
- How was it resolved?
- What are your next steps?

Of course, your questions should be concise and relevant. Asking long-winded or too many questions can be annoying. There is no formula for determining the right number of questions to ask. You'll need to rely on your intuition to guide you.

I've experienced the power of questions many times throughout my career. One memorable example occurred when I was leading a training session in New York City shortly after 9/11. After the session concluded, I headed out to meet my aunt and uncle for dinner. As I rounded the block, I could hear someone shouting. It took a few moments to realize that the source of the commotion was a man on the sidewalk about 20 yards ahead of me. Although clearly agitated, he didn't appear to be directing his anger at anyone in particular. I assumed he was under the influence of alcohol or drugs and walked past him hastily. I continued until a red light halted my progress.

As I waited for the light to change, I heard the unmistakable sound of footsteps rapidly approaching. I instinctively knew they belonged to the agitated man; when I spun around, my suspicion was confirmed. With his face almost touching mine, he bellowed, "Don't you walk away when I'm talking to you!"

I neither panicked nor lashed out. Instead, as casually as possible, I replied, "I'd be happy to hear whatever you want to say as long as you stop yelling at me."

The man paused and stepped back. His face transformed from an expression of rage to one of calm in seconds. "You're right," he said. "I apologize."

"That's OK," I replied. "Now, what would you like to say to me?"

That one question—asked with genuine interest in a non-threatening manner—changed the chords (and the course) of the entire interaction. While the exact details are fuzzy almost 25 years later, I recall that the ensuing conversation was amicable and respectful. I asked the man about his background and circumstances, and he asked me what I was doing in New York City. Erratic and aggressive only a few minutes prior, the man was now articulate and composed. It was an amazing conversion, one I would have doubted had it not happened to me.

After about 10 minutes, I shook the man's hand and wished him luck; in return, he thanked me for chatting with him. I realized later that if I'd met his aggression with aggression, his volume with volume, and his threats with threats, our exchange would have gone differently. It turns out the simple act of asking a question was the bridge two strangers needed to connect — if only for a few fleeting moments — on a busy sidewalk after one of the most traumatic days in the history of the country.

That's the power of probing. So, let me ask *you* a question: What questions can *you* ask as a leader to connect with your team?

Paraphrasing

Paraphrasing is the second *p* in our listening app. In short, paraphrasing is restating what you've heard using *your own words*. As with attending and probing, paraphrasing indicates interest and offers an opportunity to gain clarity.

Imagine your colleague shares several aspects of her work that are frustrating. To paraphrase, you might say something like: "I can understand why you'd be frustrated. It sounds like the long hours, difficult customers, and lack of understanding from your boss are taking a toll on you."

Your colleague might respond, "Yes! I'm not sure how much longer I can continue like this."

Perhaps now you follow up with a question: "Of the three issues you mentioned, is there one you find particularly difficult?"

"The customers, for sure. They drive me nuts," replies your colleague. "Is it me, or has everyone gotten more demanding and rude lately?"

You might nod empathically and respond with: "Seems that way sometimes. Tell me more. Maybe we can arrive at a solution together."

Paraphrasing accomplishes two objectives: (1) it demonstrates that you genuinely want to understand the other person, and (2) it enables you to test that your understanding is actually what the speaker meant.

An important tip: Use paraphrasing occasionally and strategically, like a chef might use an exotic herb to season a dish. Like that herb, paraphrasing can become cloying and overpowering if used too often. In those instances, your paraphrasing can feel more like interrupting than a genuine desire to communicate effectively.

The (Blessed) Sound of Silence

"Hello darkness, my old friend, I've come to talk with you again . . ."

If you're of a certain age, you most certainly recognize the opening lines of Simon & Garfunkel's famous song "The Sound of Silence." Although the album on which the song originally appeared was a commercial flop in 1964, since then "The Sound of Silence" has garnered near universal acclaim.

Part of what makes the song so appealing is the mystery surrounding the meaning of the lyrics. But while the lyrics are hauntingly ambiguous, it's the *title* that really got me thinking: What are the implications of living in a world where "the sound of silence" is increasingly rare?

I have a great sensitivity to — and little tolerance for — ambient noise (by "ambient," I mean distracting, often unavoidable sound occurring in the immediate environment). Considering I've enjoyed both listening to *and* performing loud (sometimes *very* loud) music for decades, the irony of this admission is not lost on me. Adding to the irony is that it is *music* that I typically find most offensive.

Today, music — often played at ear-splitting volume — is inescapable in malls, coffee shops, grocery stores, banks, and restaurants. But not just *any* music — music that makes me want to beat a hasty retreat toward the nearest exit.

Several months ago, I attempted to enjoy a sushi dinner with my family as the irritating bleating of "smooth jazz" saxophonist Kenny G assaulted my brain from a speaker directly over our heads. It made conversation a chore and sorely tested my patience. And unless you relish the mind-numbing *THUMP THUMP THUMP* of contemporary electronic dance music (EDM), you can forget about shopping for clothes without losing your mind (as well as your hearing).

In an NPR interview I read several years ago titled "The 'Pursuit of Silence' in a World Full of Noise," George Prochnik, author of the book *In Pursuit of Silence: Listening for*

Meaning in a World of Noise, eloquently considered the consequences of living in a noisy world:

> I work not too far away from an Abercrombie & Fitch store
> and I would hear the music booming out, and I would won-
> der what it was that was appealing to all the people, enough
> that they would want to be in an environment, spending a
> lot of time, which was often at truly eardrum-shattering lev-
> els of volume. . . .
>
> What we know is that if you're loud at this point in our cul-
> ture, it seems to signify that you're having a good time, and
> it's a fun place to be, and this is the same phenomenon that
> we find in restaurants, which continue to get louder in many
> cities every year, and many people find this unbearable. But
> many people feel that a restaurant is dead unless it has that
> noise level.

While it may not be easy to find refuge from all this noise, you
can always visit parks, libraries, art museums, hiking trails,
and other natural settings when you need a break. You should
also set aside a few minutes each day to spend in a space
devoid of noise (or at least with as little noise as possible).
Taking some time to be in stillness is good for our health, both
mental and physical, because it clears our minds of distraction and clutter, and serves as a crucial reminder that the
world will continue to spin even if we disconnect from it for a
short while. As a leader, occasionally seeking out a quiet spot
to engage in self-reflection or have a conversation with a colleague can be enormously fruitful.

Grand Finale

Communication, the first note of the CHORDS Model, is essential for effective leadership and teamwork. It is ironic that, with all the technological devices that supposedly facilitate communication at our fingertips, it remains an area many organizations continue to struggle with. While the suggestions included in this chapter are far from comprehensive, they represent a good starting point for emerging leaders. As the suggestions are foundational to success, I also believe experienced leaders — whose communication habits are likely to be more entrenched — will also benefit from adopting them.

Now It's Your Turn: Which of the ideas presented in the preceding section on Note 1 (Communication) of the CHORDS Model are resonating most? Why?

You've read the chapter — now get the tool! Dive deeper into Note 1 of the CHORDS Model by downloading "Are You an Effective Communicator?" at

rightchordleadership.com/book-resources/

Note 2: Harmony

When team members collaborate effectively, trust and morale flourish, responsibility is equally shared, and problems get solved more quickly.

According to Wikipedia, in music theory, harmony is defined as "the concept of combining different sounds together to create new, distinct musical ideas." We typically refer to notes that sound pleasant when played together as being *in harmony* or *harmonious*. For example, if the members of a church choir simultaneously sing notes that blend well, we'd say their voices are *harmonious*. However, if their voices create tension or unease within the listener, we might describe them as *dissonant*. We discussed these terms in a previous chapter.

Recall that in a work context, I use the metaphor of chords to represent the way we "show up"—how we comport ourselves and form impressions on others. Similarly, I use *harmony* metaphorically to connote a positive connection to, and relationship with, our coworkers. When we work harmoniously with others, we tend to get better results. The saying "Let's make beautiful music together" speaks to this idea. So does the tagline for my company, Right Chord Leadership: "We help leaders and teams at all levels find their groove, get in sync, and work in harmony."

One of the most impressive examples of harmony I've ever seen is a YouTube video featuring the China Disabled People's Performing Art Troupe at the 2008 Muscular Dystrophy Association telethon, hosted by the late American comedian Jerry Lewis. In his introduction, Mr. Lewis notes that the colorfully costumed troupe's members are hearing impaired.

What follows is a seven-minute, beautifully choreographed, elegantly executed display of precision movement that is truly stunning to behold. Their performance is even more extraordinary considering their disability.

I often show this video to participants in my workshops and ask, "What do you think is necessary to achieve these results?" Responses typically include cooperation, trust, reliability, commitment, dedication, and motivation. Rather than memorizing a long inventory of words, I suggest folding all of them into one, easy-to-remember concept: *harmony.*

When teams work in harmony, you can feel the energy radiating from them. Trust and morale are high; people collaborate, share ideas, and stay open to different perspectives. Because people genuinely care about each other, you'll rarely (if ever) hear "That's not my job." But you *will* frequently hear "How can I help you with that?"

Dissonant teams exhibit the opposite: They distrust one another, gossip, assume the worst of their colleagues, and engage only when necessary. I've experienced both types of teams in my career.

I was fortunate that my first job, following my pivot from advertising to learning and development (L&D) in 2001, was on a harmonious team: I worked for one year as an intern at QVC for a team called *The QVC Difference* Business Partners. During that time, I was involved in numerous projects with the Business Partners team and came to appreciate the story behind QVC's unique corporate culture.

In 1995, five years before I came onboard, former QVC president Doug Briggs had led an effort to establish a cohesive company vision and clear, unwavering values within a strong, team-oriented environment. With help from QVC's management team, an outside consulting firm, and the input of thousands of employees, Briggs developed the company's core ideology — a set of eight values known as *The QVC Difference*. At the time, Briggs asserted, "*The QVC Difference* values are our internal gyrocompass; they define how we act and give us courage and confidence in our decision making."

QVC utilized several methods to support *The QVC Difference* and integrate it into the culture. For example, the Business Partner team offered one- and two-day workshops to foster awareness and understanding among the employee population. As an intern, one of my primary responsibilities was to continually revise these workshops to make them more memorable and impactful. Admittedly, it took a while for me to feel comfortable, but this was not unexpected. As a new member of a well-established team, I knew my presence would modify the group dynamics. We needed to adjust to one another's styles, but once we did, I felt as if I'd been a team member for years.

Notably, my colleagues sought my input and opinions on projects and decisions *from the beginning*. Although I had little L&D experience, I was treated as a trusted colleague almost immediately, attending meetings with clients, developing programs, and helping to cultivate the culture of a multibillion-dollar company. My team members coached me — always respectfully and honestly — on ways to improve my performance; by the time my internship concluded, I was a far more capable and confident L&D practitioner than before. We experienced high levels of trust, camaraderie, collaboration, and morale, which fostered our productivity. If someone had to leave early, for example, another would gladly stay and pick up the slack. If someone promised to complete a piece of work by a certain deadline, we knew he or she would, no questions asked. That team was a well-oiled machine fueled by the harmonious chords we played every day.

In October 2002, after I'd accepted a full-time position at QVC, a member of the organizational development (OD) team asked if I would be interested in doing some work for them. We agreed that I'd assist in the development of a training program for mid-level managers called "Building Effective Teams: Developing Your Management Style." I was disappointed with this project. The work was lackluster and progressed slowly. I was further challenged working with the OD team for the first time and needing to understand their individual styles and work habits. It wasn't that my teammates were difficult; on the contrary, everyone was good-natured and competent. It's just that the *harmony*—that sense of energy, enthusiasm, and forward movement I'd enjoyed as an intern—was absent.

I realized later that I was partly to blame for the dissonance I felt. In hindsight, I should have requested a clearer explanation of the project's objectives up front, as well as inclusion in initial discussions. Although my feelings of disenchantment subsided as I got more comfortable in the role, the lack of harmony I experienced during those first few months made for a rocky start.

Better Teamwork Through Harmony

A friend and I were recently engaged in an online conversation about who would appear on our "Mt. Rushmore of Rock" in the following categories: singer, guitar, bass, and drums (I admit we are both total music geeks).

By "Mt. Rushmore of Rock," we meant the four individuals in *each* category whose significance, influence, notoriety, and skill put them on a higher level than their peers. After I completed my list, my friend noticed that I'd included all four members of Led Zeppelin in their respective categories: Robert Plant for singer, Jimmy Page for guitar, John Paul Jones for bass, and the late John "Bonzo" Bonham for drums.

"Pretty amazing to include all four guys from Zeppelin," my friend wrote. "It confirms that they are clearly the greatest band of all time."

"With Zep, it was all about team harmony," I responded. "The piercing wail of Plant's voice, the testosterone-fueled crunch of Page's guitar, the chunky thump of Jones's bass, and the crushing thunder of Bonzo's drum kit made for a one-of-a-kind sound that set the stage for thousands of bands that followed."

This nerdy little exercise got me pondering the nature of team harmony in general — what it is, why it matters, and how to cultivate it. I can't help but think there is something about team harmony that eludes explanation, some intangible quality no definition, model, or theory fully captures. As a musician, I would call it a sense of being in sync with one another. You can't see or touch it, but you can sure *feel* it. In Zeppelin's case, harmony manifested as that one-of-a-kind, instantly identifiable *sound* that could only be produced by *those four musicians* together and no others.

How does harmony show up on *your* team? Some teams just click right away: Call it *instant harmony*. For others, it may take some work, while some never get there at all. As a leader, you play a vital role in sustaining harmony and fending off dissonance on your team.

Now that you have a better understanding of what harmony and dissonance are in an organizational context, let's focus on what the *best* leaders do to develop harmonious teams.

A thorough examination of the factors that contribute to team harmony would require its own book. However, I will share a few important ones here that any leader looking to cultivate a high-performance team should consider.

Behavioral Styles

Understanding and accepting people's behavioral styles is one of the most obvious hallmarks of harmonious teams. The popular DiSC® profile, for example, classifies people into four styles known by their first letter: D for Dominance, i for Influence, S for Steadiness, and C for Conscientiousness. Each style is associated with distinct characteristics and tendencies:

- **D—Dominance**. Characterized by control, power, and assertiveness. Individuals who score high in dominance focus on achieving results and are typically confident, opinionated, emphatic, and resolute.

- **i—Influence**. Characterized by extroversion and sociability. Individuals who rank high in this style are skilled at influencing or persuading others and tend to be optimistic, animated, and active.
- **S—Steadiness**. Characterized by patience, thoughtfulness, and empathy. Individuals who score high in steadiness are typically cooperative, sincere, and excellent listeners.
- **C—Conscientiousness**. Characterized by uniformity and structure. Individuals who score high in conscientiousness emphasize accuracy, order, detail, and precision.

In my teambuilding workshops, I divide participants up by letter—the D's in one corner, the i's in another corner, and so on. Each team is challenged to develop and act out a 30-second TV commercial for Coke that appeals to its so-called *opposing style* as follows:

- The D's create a commercial that appeals to the S's and vice versa
- The i's create a commercial that appeals to the C's and vice versa

This exercise forces participants to think in a way that is foreign to them:

- The D's must adopt the mindset of an S (cooperative, sincere, dependable, calm, empathic)
- The S's need to adopt the mindset of a D (assertive, confident, decisive, outspoken)

- The i's need to adopt the mindset of a C (organized, logical, meticulous, detail-oriented)
- The C's need to adopt the mindset of an i (outgoing, sociable, fun-loving, expressive)

As you'd expect, hilarity ensues as each group attempts to appeal to a wildly different disposition than their own. More importantly, attendees come away with a heightened sense of the differences among the four styles. Note that one style is *not* better or worse than another; *all four are necessary* for a high-performance workplace because each has its own strengths and liabilities. One of the keys to cultivating a harmonious team is not only to be aware of these stylistic differences but to leverage them in a way that fosters rather than hinders productivity. *Whether or not that happens is everybody's responsibility, but the leader plays an outsized role.*

Adapting more effectively to different styles can reduce conflict in the workplace dramatically, while recognizing the strengths and liabilities of *your own style* increases self-awareness. If your team hasn't taken the DiSC assessment, I heartily recommend it. As U2 singer Bono said, "To be one, to be united, is a great thing. But to respect the right to be different is maybe even greater."

Adaptability

Another factor that impacts team harmony is adaptability. Consider ants, worms, and rats for a moment (but only if you're willing, of course). Lowly creatures, right? But they all have something in common: *they are three of the most adaptable creatures on the planet.* They can survive harsh conditions that other animals could never survive. Like these animals, the ability to adapt is critical for humans as well.

You may be wondering what adaptability means exactly. Adaptability speaks to our ability to adjust to different environments, people, and circumstances. For example, things may be a certain way one day and completely different the next. You lose a job. You get a pay raise. A close friend leaves the country. You find out you're having a baby. A family member passes away. Despite our best attempts to plan for the future, life is ultimately unpredictable.

Think of the last time you had to adapt to an unexpected occurrence or a new, unfamiliar situation. Was it easy or difficult? *Our circumstances in life are always changing. Even the smallest of events and circumstances can radically disrupt your life.* I remember when I left my last corporate job in 2007 and went out on my own. Talk about a huge change! I had no choice but to adapt to my new circumstances that included no steady paycheck. At first, I thought I'd erred in leaving my employer, but soon my entrepreneurial spirit kicked into high gear, and I accepted the challenges facing me with confidence and enthusiasm. I ate a lot of cold cereal for dinner out of necessity, but I somehow found the drive and conviction to persevere.

Adaptable leaders and teams possess certain key qualities:

- Receptivity to learning from experience, which in turn opens doors to more opportunities
- Openness to change even if the outcome is unclear

- Resilience during unstable or unpredictable times
- Willingness to rethink what they believe is "right" and experiment with new ways of doing things

Adaptable leaders and teams see possibilities where others see failure and are more resourceful than those who don't or can't adapt successfully. They think ahead and are on the lookout for ways to improve. They're not married to one-size-fits-all solutions but look instead for different ways to accomplish goals. They identify the habits that have gotten them to where they are today and consider whether those same habits will be helpful in the future. They have contingency plans in place for when Plan A doesn't work. Perhaps most importantly, they *listen* to alternative—and even opposing—points of view and respect different opinions *even if they disagree.*

In short, adaptable leaders and team members realize the only constant in life is change. Consequently, they view change as an opportunity rather than a threat. As a leader, your ability to not only accept change but adapt to it is a vital quality for achieving success.

Interlude: Made a Mistake? How Fascinating!

The preceding discussion on adaptability reminds me of a story about two legendary jazz musicians: trumpeter Miles Davis and pianist Herbie Hancock. Together, they recorded some of the greatest jazz in history. But it's not their music I want to examine here. Instead, I want to share a story about

Miles, as told by Herbie, that beautifully captures the importance of adaptability to effective leadership. Even if you don't care for jazz, I think the lesson will resonate with you.

In a YouTube video titled "Miles Davis according to Herbie Hancock," Herbie relates an incident that occurred during a concert with the Miles Davis Quintet in the '60s featuring the late saxophonist Wayne Shorter, bassist Ron Carter, Miles on trumpet, the late Tony Williams on drums, and Herbie on piano. Here's a piece of that interview:

> Right in the middle of [Miles's] solo, I played the wrong chord . . . a chord that just sounded completely wrong. It sounded like a big mistake. . . . And Miles paused for a second and then he played some notes that made my chord right, made it correct, which astounded me. I couldn't believe what I heard. Miles was able to make something that was wrong into something that was right with the power of the choice of notes that he made and the feeling that he had. . . . Miles didn't hear [my wrong chord] as a mistake. He heard it as something that happened, just an event. . . . [Miles] felt it was his responsibility to find something that fit.

As the band leader, Miles could have easily humiliated Herbie for playing the incorrect chord (as great a player as Miles was, he could be nasty). Instead, he chose to turn Herbie's "mistake" into a surprising musical moment that not only saved Herbie from embarrassment but took the band in an unexpected musical direction.

To be clear, I'm not advocating that leaders *encourage* mistakes. Nor am I proposing that leaders celebrate egregious mistakes born of incompetence or sloppiness. Rather, I'm suggesting that leaders always have a *choice* when mistakes are made (and they undoubtedly will be). I believe leaders who inspire greatness in others constantly adapt, adjust, and recalibrate. They deal with mistakes *without placing blame or finger-pointing*. Most of the people I've worked with over my career identify their worst bosses as those who instilled a *fear of mistakes* and sought retribution when they occurred.

The incident described above reminds me of something another musical titan, Boston Philharmonic conductor Benjamin Zander, once said in an interview with *USA Today*:

> I think it's tremendously important to develop a powerful relationship with failure. If you're a coward and stopped by failure there's no way to develop. Making mistakes is the most valuable training there is. My teacher used to say you can't play great music unless your heart has been broken. So maybe the answer is to have more broken hearts and get on with it. That's why I teach my students to celebrate mistakes. Every time they make mistakes I say, "How fascinating!"

Once again, permit me to stress that adopting a "How fascinating!" mindset when a catastrophic error occurs will not serve you. Short of that, however, leaders who believe mistakes and failures are how we get better are universally respected. My old music teachers knew it. Miles Davis knew it. Benjamin Zander knows it. And you should too.

Developing Adaptability

To develop adaptability, consider the following behaviors:

Stop whining and complaining. What is your habitual response when something negative happens? Do you think "I'll handle it" or "Why does this stuff always happen to me?" Many people start whining as soon as they find themselves in a difficult situation. This is a common reaction that leads nowhere. If you're one of these people, try changing the language you use. Adaptable people don't whine, blame fate, or constantly complain. If they can't change or influence a decision, they *adapt* and move on without holding grudges or bringing down those around them.

Adaptable people don't waste time wishing things were different; they get to work solving the problem or making the best of tough circumstances. They don't blame themselves for mistakes, failures, or rejections either. They realize that if they can't change something, they *must* accept it and do the best they can.

Engage in positive self-talk. You don't need to have a long conversation with yourself every morning, but occasional positive self-talk can help you adapt to changes more quickly. Simple statements like "I can do this" or "This too will pass" (one of my grandmother's favorite sayings) can be helpful. As the late Desmond Tutu once said, "Language is very powerful. Language does not just describe reality. *Language creates the reality it describes* [italics added]." That's why positive self-talk is so powerful.

Be open to change. Change, like conflict, isn't necessarily bad. In fact, change often makes our lives better. Think of all the positive changes you've experienced in your life. I bet you can name many of them. Unless you're doing something that can hurt yourself or others, I suggest adopting a mindset where you lean into change rather than resist it. Consider the earlier Miles Davis anecdote: Miles didn't *reject* Herbie's wrong chord; he accepted it and, in Herbie's words, "turned poison into medicine."

Have a plan but be flexible. Success is rarely, if ever, a straight line. So while it's important to have a plan for what you want to accomplish, it's equally important to be flexible. Adaptable people realize this and never stop adjusting to whatever life throws at them. I'm reminded of a great quote from famed martial artist and movie star Bruce Lee: "You put water into a cup, it *becomes* the cup. You put water into a bottle, it *becomes* the bottle. You put it in a teapot, it *becomes* the teapot . . . Be water, my friend." To me, this quote is an exhortation to be agile, nimble, and flexible no matter what situation or circumstance we may be facing.

If you want to become more adaptable, you need to start changing your orientation to change. Yes, change can be disruptive and difficult, but the way you think about and deal with change can make all the difference. If you resist change, you're going to end up exhausted. But if you remain open to change and do your best to navigate it successfully, you may find some wonderful things on the other side.

Interlude: Rock of Ages

Def Leppard, the '80s pop metal band whose albums *Pyromania* and *Hysteria* each sold in the tens of millions and catapulted them to global stardom, almost lost everything just as they were achieving massive success.

On New Year's Eve in 1984, drummer Rick Allen crashed his car near the band's hometown of Sheffield, UK, and lost his left arm when his seat belt severed it. Rather than curl up in a self-pitying ball, Allen was determined to recover quickly and get back in the studio. A friend of his (who was adept at electronics) designed a custom electronic drum kit that Allen could play with his feet. Furthermore, the band never considered replacing Allen and granted him as much time as he needed to regain his health. Since then, Def Leppard has continued to put out albums and tour relentlessly, a testament to their resolve and intense love for each other.

A few years ago, on the anniversary of Allen's near-fatal accident, his tale of resilience got me thinking about adaptability: Why are some people more adaptable than others? Think about all the ways people had to adapt after Allen lost his arm:

- Allen had to adapt to an entirely new drum kit and method of playing drums.
- Allen's friend had to adapt the electronic kit to the drummer's unique physical needs.
- The band had to adapt to the reality of a severely injured drummer and make some huge decisions regarding his (and their) future.

Imagine the tenacity required by all parties to push past that tragedy, return to the studio, and record one of their most successful albums (1987's *Hysteria*). Consider the positive self-talk necessary to get to that point, the openness and receptivity to radical change and bold solutions, and the planning involved to not only retain their drummer but come back as a unit stronger than ever. Truly inspiring stuff!

No matter what you think of Def Leppard's music, theirs is unquestionably a story of triumph over adversity from which all leaders can learn.

Engagement

You've likely heard the term "employee engagement," another key element to developing and sustaining a harmonious team. While it's not a new idea, many definitions exist, making it challenging to characterize precisely. In short, employee engagement — or simply *engagement* — is the emotional commitment an employee has to their work. When an employee is "engaged," he or she cares about their company and their output *beyond merely earning a paycheck*. Engaged employees expend *discretionary effort* — effort above and beyond what is required to do their job well enough not to get fired.

An engaged receptionist, for example, might offer visitors a drink, ask about their day, point out the restrooms, or keep them apprised of any delays. An engaged salesperson might attempt to squeeze in one more call before the end of the day, after her colleagues have gone home. An engaged sales associate working in a retail store might greet customers warmly, ask if there is anything he or she can do to help, and personally walk customers over to items of interest.

Engaged employees feel a sense of *ownership* regarding their work (the third note in the CHORDS Model, which we'll explore next). They execute their job duties with zeal and take pride in their contributions. That doesn't mean they're happy every moment of every day. Rather, it means they're motivated, have a sense of purpose, and are committed to the mission, vision, and values of the company.

The research on employee engagement is clear: Engaged employees simply perform better than disengaged employees. Disengaged employees are *less* likely to put in effort, feel motivated, or meet their role's expectations. They produce more errors in their work and can adversely impact the morale of a team that is otherwise engaged. On the other hand, engaged teams enjoy higher levels of productivity and lower absenteeism, provide better service, and generally have a more satisfying experience at work.

If employees are having a miserable time and playing notes that are "out of tune," your customers will surely know it. What's more, their poor attitude will create an environment where people dread working. Burnout, decreased morale, and high levels of turnover will inevitably result. Not exactly playing the right chords!

The percentages of engaged versus disengaged employees vary depending on what study you read. Frankly, I don't think the numbers are that important. What matters is understanding what engagement is, why it's essential, and most importantly, how you as a leader can help create and sustain it. Now that we've addressed the first two issues, let's turn to the third.

The Progress Principle

What is the so-called "secret sauce" for creating engagement on your team? Thanks to years of robust research, the ingredients are well-known. You're probably familiar with many of them: show appreciation, provide clear goals, create a pleasant work environment, and so on. However, several years ago, Harvard Business Review Press published a book on engagement and performance you may not be acquainted with. Cowritten by Harvard Business School professor Dr. Teresa Amabile and Dr. Steven Kramer, *The Progress Principle: Using Small Wins to Ignite Joy, Engagement, and Creativity at Work* presents the findings from a comprehensive study on the factors that boost or hinder engagement in the workplace. I believe what Drs. Amabile and Kramer discovered should be in *every* leader's playbook if they're striving to develop an engaged workforce.

One of the key concepts explored in *The Progress Principle* is *inner work life*, which the authors define as "the perceptions, emotions, and motivations that people experience as they react to and make sense of events in the workday." You can't see a person's inner work life, of course. Amabile and Kramer write, "Inner work life is the mostly invisible part of each individual's experience—the thoughts, feelings, and drives triggered by the events of the workday."

As you would expect, when employees feel valued, derive pride and satisfaction from their work, and feel suitably challenged, inner work life increases. Consequently, employees will be more productive, collaborative, and motivated. However, when people *don't* feel valued and/or take little or no pride in their work, inner work life suffers. In such cases, employees tend to expend the minimum amount of effort not to get fired *and no more*. Furthermore, because their work is executed without emotional investment, carelessness in the guise of accidents and mistakes proliferates. Disengaged individuals go to work merely to earn a paycheck; for them, each day is a slog to get through.

You may know such an individual at your own organization. If so, you probably understand how much their attitude can negatively impact an entire team. If the poor inner work life of just *one person* can have such an outsized effect, imagine a *team* full of disengaged employees. I've seen instances where even a few "checked out" employees have brought down an entire department by turning it toxic.

Since we've established that employees do better work when they possess a *positive* inner work life, it's only natural to consider exactly *what* elevates employees' inner work lives.

Amabile and Kramer provide some insight. Their research involved 238 knowledge workers — employees who primarily work with information or knowledge rather than engage in physical labor — on 26 project teams in 7 companies in 3 industries. By analyzing nearly 12,000 individual daily diary forms sent to study participants, the authors discovered that, of all the positive events that can boost inner work life, *the single most powerful is making progress in meaningful work.*

This is the Progress Principle. Amabile and Kramer write, "Progress triggers positive emotions, leads to a sense of accomplishment and self-worth as well as positive views of the work and the organization. Such thoughts and perceptions (along with those positive emotions) feed the motivation, the deep engagement, that is crucial for ongoing blockbuster performance."

Although all this seems simple enough, there's a lot to unpack. Let's start with the authors' basic premise, the notion that making progress is the number one driver of engagement and performance in the workplace. Later, we'll tackle the "meaningful work" piece of the Progress Principle.

What is it about *progress* that makes it such a potent driver of workplace engagement? Consider that making progress appeals to one of our most fundamental human drives: the drive toward self-efficacy. The authors define self-efficacy as "a person's belief that he or she is individually capable of planning and executing the tasks required to achieve desired goals." In other words, each time we make progress on a task or set of tasks, *we feel a sense of accomplishment*. This makes us feel good about ourselves and inspires us to tackle the next task.

Think about how much of our lives revolves around making progress. Whether we're learning a musical instrument, competing in a sport, writing a book, or pursuing an academic degree, making progress makes us feel capable and competent. When we make progress, our faith in ourselves and our ability to tackle tough challenges increases; we feel empowered, encouraged, and energized.

Conversely, when we *fail* to make progress, we may experience self-doubt, uncertainty, and insecurity. Our motivation to continue may dissipate like air slowly leaking from a balloon. After multiple setbacks, we may give up entirely, and our sense of self-efficacy and of self-worth may be permanently damaged.

By now, the impact of progress — or the *lack* of progress — on our psychological well-being should be clear. Unfortunately, the research suggests it's not clear to many managers.

Leading Using the Progress Principle

When Amabile and Kramer discovered the Progress Principle, they designed a follow-up survey to test managers' understanding of it. Nearly 670 managers were asked to rank the importance of five workplace motivators:

1. Recognition
2. Incentives
3. Interpersonal support
4. Clear goals
5. Support for making progress

Guess which one came in *last*.

If you chose "support for making progress," you're right. In fact, *only 5 percent of the managers surveyed ranked making progress as the number one motivator*. This result is stunning considering the authors found progress to be the *number one motivator* of workplace engagement and performance. Amabile and Kramer write, "Our results reveal unawareness of the power of progress across all levels of management. Any manager's job description should start with facilitating subordinates' progress every day. *Even if this imperative isn't big news for you, many managers are clearly unaware of it* [italics added]."

It's important to note that progress comes in many forms. Of course, major breakthroughs and big leaps forward are types of progress, but they don't occur often during a typical workday. More common are so-called "small wins," seemingly minor moments of progress such as completing a task or taking a small step forward on a large project.

Here's the good news for leaders: The authors discovered that *small wins can have significant inner work life benefits, sometimes as notable as much more impressive leaps forward.* This means when an employee makes progress at work, managers should refrain from trivializing or minimizing it. Managers need not throw a giant celebration, but they should at least *acknowledge* it. Something as simple as "I know how hard you've been working, and I appreciate it" may be enough to leverage the Progress Principle and make employees feel good about themselves.

On the downside, Amabile and Kramer found that even *seemingly minor setbacks* can set inner work life back. If you've ever experienced a setback at work, you know how strongly it can affect your mood and motivation. Managers who recognize that inner work life rises and falls with progress and setbacks have a distinct advantage over their peers. Managers may not be able to prevent *all* setbacks, but they can at least help employees address and try to overcome them. In short, they can use their position of authority to help people make progress as well as navigate setbacks. As Amabile and Kramer write, "A review of your people's progress should become a daily discipline."

Let's now focus on the "meaningful work" part of the Progress Principle. Without a sense that one's work *matters*—that it is making a consequential difference—engagement and performance falter.

With some jobs, the meaning of the work is obvious. Think about the work of firefighters, scientists, teachers, nurses, and the U.S. military, just to name a few examples. If you were asked to name the *meaning* of these jobs, you would need only a few seconds to respond. While the meaning of *these* jobs is clear, however, the meaning of many other types of jobs is not nearly as profound.

And that's OK.

According to Amabile and Kramer, one's work doesn't need to have enormous importance to society to be meaningful—*what matters is whether the worker perceives their work as contributing value to something or someone who matters.* Consequently, meaning can be derived from many sources, such as

- Making a useful and high-quality product for customers,
- Providing an important service to one's own community,
- Working with a boss or colleague whom you like and trust, or
- Providing sustenance for one's family.

Whether work goals are lofty or modest, if they are meaningful *to the individual doing the work*, the Progress Principle can be leveraged. That means even routine work can have meaning for those doing it. Whether it's making sandwiches, collecting trash, or styling hair, *to cultivate an engaged workforce, it's vital for employees to feel that their work has meaning.* Leaders should therefore ensure the meaning of their team's work is unambiguous and issue frequent reminders about its value.

Negating the meaning of an employee's work is one of the quickest ways to decrease engagement and, subsequently, impair performance. It is vital that managers make sure their people know just how their work is contributing and, most importantly, avoid actions that negate the value of the work. In one of my first jobs as an advertising copywriter, I spent weeks working with the agency's art director to create a series of print ads for one of our most prestigious clients. The head of the agency planned to visit this client with the ads in tow, and we hustled to get the work done prior to his departure. When he returned, we asked how the ads were received. He replied that he hadn't shared them because "there wasn't enough time."

Imagine how dejected we felt after all the hours we'd spent creating those ads. This incident happened almost 30 years ago, and I can still remember it clearly. As a leader, you should *always* treat people and their work with respect and dignity.

Each of us needs to believe our work is contributing to something consequential. When that belief is strong, progress leads to genuine satisfaction, strong motivation, and positive feelings. But when our work feels devoid of meaning, even completing a long list of tasks won't be fulfilling. Consider my short stint as a sporting goods store employee when I was in high school. My job consisted of organizing the various items on the shelves, occasionally checking customers out, and putting those small, rectangular price stickers with the purple ink on every item (ask someone older if you don't know what I'm talking about). That last task was the worst. Every bowling ball, batting glove, football helmet, hockey stick, and jock strap in the store required a price sticker. Sure, I made daily progress affixing those stickers onto each item. But was I engaged? Enthusiastic? Invested in my work? Hell no.

Imagine the difference if I'd had a manager who understood the Progress Principle. They might have said, "Mike, I know putting price stickers on merchandise isn't the most thrilling job. But it's critical to our success that it's done efficiently and accurately. Each error requires time to investigate and fix — time that could be spent helping customers. If you need a break, feel free to take one, or let me know and I'll put you on the register. I sincerely appreciate your attention to detail. Keep it up."

Now *that's* how you derive meaning from a menial task!

Engaging Remotely

While the Progress Principle applies to any team of knowledge workers, remote teams are a special case. With many employees now working from home at least part time after the COVID-19 pandemic, remote work has skyrocketed in popularity. But the need for engaged team members hasn't changed; in fact, it's become even *more* crucial.

Without the in-person watercooler conversations, spontaneous breakroom discussions, staff retreats, and after-work get-togethers that fostered collaboration and camaraderie pre-pandemic, people can feel disconnected nowadays. Leaders need to be especially patient, compassionate, and sensitive to their coworkers' needs. Ensuring remote team members are engaged not just with their work but with their fellow team members is of paramount importance.

Here are some proven ways to keep remote employees engaged:

- **Express more appreciation than usual.** When opportunities for in-person recognition are limited, it's easy to overlook how much people value acknowledgment and appreciation. While grand gestures aren't necessary, simply recognizing good work can make a significant impact.
- **Check in with staff regularly.** There is a fine line between routinely checking in with your team members (individually and collectively) and being a nuisance, so don't overdo it. These shouldn't be opportunities to check *up on* people ("Are you getting your work done?") as much as to check *in with* people ("What challenges are you facing, and how can I help you?").
- **Take the pulse of your team.** Employee engagement surveys are great, but simply sending out short "pulse checks" every quarter can also help you better understand how engaged employees are and which issues may need your attention.
- **Leverage the Progress Principle.** Track employees' progress over time. Take note of goals, performance metrics, and individual development. These should be

documented and shared with each employee individually to ensure you're both on the same page.

- **Create cross-departmental projects or organize brainstorming sessions that encourage free thinking and spontaneous idea generation.** One-on-ones are obviously helpful, but meetings where team members problem solve together can foster open communication and collaboration that mimic office culture.
- **Encourage questions and frank discussions during virtual meetings.** The breakout room feature in Zoom is especially good for fostering candid dialogue as it allows small groups to chat before convening the full team.

There's no magic to achieving an engaged workforce. It comes down to a few simple principles that, when practiced regularly, will help you get the best from your team. As a leader, it's your job to help your teammates make progress, overcome setbacks, and find meaning in their work; remind them that their efforts are valued and appreciated; celebrate wins (big and small); and keep the whole team connected, whether they're in-person or remote.

Grand Finale

To win in the marketplace, you must first win in the workplace. Achieving harmony among a multitude of temperaments, personalities, styles, attitudes, motivations, and agendas isn't easy. However, I am confident the suggestions provided in this chapter will help propel your team to new heights of excellence.

Now It's Your Turn: Which of the ideas presented in this chapter are resonating most? Why?

You've read the chapter—now get the tool! Take the next step in your leadership journey by downloading "Better Teamwork Through Harmony" at

rightchordleadership.com/book-resources/

Note 3: Ownership

When employees possess a sense of ownership, they exhibit
accountability, exude pride in their work, and go the extra mile
for the customer and each other.

How many times have you heard someone say, "We need to *hold* him accountable" or "They need to be *held* accountable" *after* a misdeed has been committed? In other words, someone messed up, and now, after the fact, those in charge are going to punish them accordingly. This is the context in which *accountable* is typically used. No wonder the notion of accountability strikes fear and anxiety in many of us.

In his book *Winning With Accountability: The Secret Language of High-Performing Organizations*, author Henry J. Evans suggests accountability is characteristically viewed as punitive, something people associate with things going wrong. This is a misguided way to think about accountability. He writes:

> In reality, winning begins with accountability. You cannot sustain success without accountability. It is an absolute requirement. The secret that successful organizations have discovered is to install accountability on the front end of interactions . . . before the outcome is known. Successful organizations front-load accountability into their strategy. When front-loaded, accountability breeds better relationships, eliminates surprises, and vastly improves job satisfaction and performance.

I believe Evans is correct. Many of us associate accountability with "getting caught with our hand in the cookie jar and now having to pay the piper" (there, I gave you two outdated metaphors for the price of one). In other words, we were naughty and must now face the consequences. It's unfortunate that accountability has acquired such a negative connotation because without it, your team will never play the right chords and produce outstanding results.

Accountability Versus Responsibility

Let's begin our discussion of accountability by contrasting it with another familiar word: responsibility. *Responsibility* and *accountability* are often used interchangeably even though they mean different things.

My definition of responsibility: *Agreeing to complete the tasks and duties associated with one's role or position.*

Want some examples? Police officers are *responsible* for protecting and serving their community. Attorneys are *responsible* for representing their clients to the best of their abilities. Someone on your team might volunteer to *take responsibility* for organizing the company softball game. You get the idea. In short, you accept responsibility *before* a job, task, or undertaking is started.

My definition of accountability: *Making a personal choice to answer for — in other words, to own — the outcomes of one's decisions, behaviors, and actions (or those of others if you're a leader).*

As you can see, the key idea with accountability is *ownership*, which is the third note in the CHORDS Model. Ownership is something you accept *after* the job, task, or undertaking is completed. That's a crucial distinction. Imagine promising your boss you'll stay late to finish a report she needs for a 9 a.m. meeting the next morning. However, your friend calls at 6:30 p.m. and invites you to meet a group of friends for dinner. Dining out sounds way more fun than working on the report, so you agree. "I'll just finish it when I get in tomorrow," you decide. "Besides, she doesn't need it until 9 a.m."

Unbeknownst to you, however, your boss elects to move her meeting from 9 a.m. to 8 a.m. (Remember, she thinks you're finishing the report *that evening*.) When 7:45 a.m. rolls around, she calls to ask about the report.

"I thought your meeting wasn't until 9 a.m.," you stammer.

"I switched some things around and moved it an hour earlier," she retorts. "Did you finish the report last night like you promised?"

"I decided to finish it when I got in this morning," you reply sheepishly. "Something came up last minute."

"Well, I'm meeting with the CFO in 15 minutes, and he's going to ask for it."

"I wish you'd told me the meeting was moved up an hour. I would have—"

Your boss cuts you off. "To be frank, you told me you'd finish it last night. I was counting on you. Now I'm going to have to make up an excuse as to why it's not finished. He won't be happy."

Just writing that fictional scenario gives me a knot in my stomach. What happened here? You accepted responsibility for completing the report, but you didn't hold up your end of the bargain. You didn't do what you said you would. And instead of apologizing profusely for your poor judgment and pledging never to do it again, you deflected blame onto your boss by suggesting *she* should have informed you about the schedule change. You're refusing to take accountability. In short, you're not accepting *ownership* of your actions, making a bad situation even worse.

Any way you slice it, it's a bad look for you. But it's also a bad look for your boss. She now must go to *her* boss, the CFO, and explain what happened. You've made your boss look irresponsible at best, inept at worst.

I hope that meal was worth it.

Ownership in the workplace is crucial at *all* job levels, but it's especially important for leaders to model. Few things erode a culture as quickly as leaders demanding accountability from their people while failing to act accountably themselves. At one of my accountability workshops, for example, a young woman told me — with an unmistakable note of weariness in her voice — that she'd recently raised a concern with her boss only to be told to "stay in her own lane." Such an abrupt dismissal of an employee's legitimate concern should be an exhibit in the "Terrible Leadership Hall of Fame." The irony of this employee attending an accountability workshop *rather than her boss* was not lost on either of us. Unfortunately, this sort of thing happens all the time.

Let's explore the definition of accountability (i.e., ownership) a bit further. Consider a football team (if you're reading this outside of the U.S., I'm talking *American* football). Which members of the team are *responsible* for the play on the field — the tackling, passing, kicking, blocking, and so on? The players, of course. But at the end of a losing season, which team member is hauled in front of the press and compelled to explain through clenched teeth why the team performed so poorly?

The coach.

It's worth noting that the coach never threw a pass, blocked an opposing player, or kicked a field goal (hopefully not, anyway). Yet they are ultimately *accountable*—literally, *held to account*—for the team's results. They *own* those results. As such, you as a leader can be *accountable* for an employee's actions without necessarily being *responsible* for them. It may not be fair, but that's part of being a leader.

As a long-time resident of the Philadelphia suburbs, I used to hear former Philadelphia Eagles head coach Andy Reid take accountability for his team's poor performance after every loss. He'd say, "I've got to do a better job of getting our team ready" and "We've got to do better, starting with me." But when the team continued to lose, Reid's responses became meaningless, even laughable. The point is that *admissions of accountability mean little if results don't change.* While taking ownership without blaming others is important, making the necessary changes to improve outcomes is equally so.

Here's another example to underscore this crucial point. Several years ago, an incident at a Starbucks in Philadelphia made national news. Two African American men were waiting for a colleague to arrive. They hadn't ordered anything and were allegedly told by a Starbucks employee to "make a purchase or leave." A commotion ensued, and the two men were arrested after the store manager called 911. Shortly after the incident, former Starbucks CEO Kevin Johnson went on CNN to apologize: "These two gentlemen did not deserve what happened. And we are accountable. *I am accountable.*"

That's a great example of taking accountability for, or owning, something you were not directly responsible for. Consider that Johnson wasn't in Starbucks at the time of the incident. *He* wasn't the one who insisted the men place an order. *He* didn't call 911 or have them arrested. In short, he wasn't responsible. Yet, as the company CEO, he stepped up and took *accountability* for the actions of his employees. He *owned* the results of their behavior. That alone is commendable.

But what Johnson did next elevated him in my eyes even further. After the incident, he ordered more than 8,000 stores closed for racial bias training. He could have stopped at "I am accountable" and continued business as usual. But by taking the extra step, he demonstrated a strong commitment to changing his company's policies and protocols to avoid a similar situation in the future.

That's what ownership looks and sounds like.

Another famous incident concerning accountability occurred in June 2010 during a baseball game between the Detroit Tigers and the Cleveland Indians (now Guardians). Tigers pitcher Armando Galarraga was robbed *one out short* of a perfect game when first base umpire Jim Joyce erred in calling the batter safe after a ground ball (replays showed the batter was *clearly* out). Upon reviewing the play after the game, a tearful Joyce admitted not getting the call correct: "I took a perfect game away from that kid." Galarraga was forgiving, telling reporters "Nobody's perfect. Everyone makes mistakes." Joyce's display of accountability, as well as Galarraga's sportsmanship, were widely praised.

That's what ownership looks and sounds like.

In a more recent example of exhibiting accountability, pop star Taylor Swift posted the following on her social media accounts after cutting her hand at an April 2023 show in Houston: "Loving this tour so much because of the passion these crowds put into it all—seriously can't wait for Atlanta. PS for those asking how I cut my hand, I'm totally fine and it was my fault completely—tripped on my dress hem and fell in the dark backstage while running to a quick change—braced my fall with my palm." I'm not a Taylor Swift fan, but I appreciate her honest admission. She could have blamed any number of assistants, technicians, engineers, or crew members for the mishap. Instead, in a rare showing of grace and humility for such a popular celebrity, she did the right thing.

That's what accountability looks and sounds like.

Unfortunately, I think these examples represent the exception rather than the rule. It's far easier to find instances of leaders *not* taking ownership—pointing fingers, placing blame, making excuses, and deflecting attention away from their mistakes.

The Wells Fargo banking scandal of 2016 stands out to me as a particularly egregious example of unaccountable leadership. To simplify a complex story, Wells Fargo put enormous pressure on employees to hit sales quotas, leading to unethical behavior, such as getting fired for reporting misconduct. An independent investigation identified cultural, structural, and leadership issues as root causes of the improper sales practices.

Shortly after the scandal broke, CEO John Stumpf blamed a few bad employees who didn't honor the company's values and asserted there were no incentives to commit unethical behavior (a claim later proven false). Let's be clear here: What Stumpf did is not leadership. It is cowardice. The pervasiveness of such behavior is a tragic indictment of the business community, but one can easily find similarly reprehensible behavior in our academic, political, and social institutions as well. Unfortunately, many of those in power escape justice by letting underlings and subordinates take the fall. The lesson seems to be that owning the results of one's actions is for chumps while denial, deflection, distraction, and delay pay handsomely.

While it is true that powerful leaders often avoid accountability, a quote attributed to former NFL head coach Bum Philips is just as true: "You fail all the time, but you aren't a failure until you start blaming someone else." I can't think of a more succinct rationale for leaders to model accountable behavior.

Own Your Own Mistakes

Playing music professionally for almost 40 years has taught me the importance of owning my results. I realize that when we think of accountable people, the first examples that pop into mind are likely not musicians. That's understandable. If you're a classic rock fan like me, you're no doubt familiar with legendary tales of debauchery and mischief from bands such as Led Zeppelin, The Who, and Guns N' Roses. If you're a jazz fan, you may have read about the reckless behavior of icons such as Charlie Parker and Miles Davis. Similarly, there is no shortage of tales of classical composers behaving badly —

from long nights of heavy drinking to vulgar pranks to fits of rage. Hell, even Justin Bieber has a criminal record.

As a member of numerous musical groups over the years, I've learned the best musicians are both *responsible* for learning their parts and playing them correctly as well as *accountable* when things don't go as planned. Back in the '90s, I forgot to bring my saxophone strap to a gig because I'd used it earlier to practice at home and failed to put it back in the case. When I arrived at the venue, I opened the case and began to search frantically for the strap (a tenor sax is too heavy to play without one). Consider my options at that point. I could have blamed my wife for not reminding me to take it (*really* bad idea). I could have lapsed into victim behavior: "Why do these things always happen *to me*?" I could have told my bandmates, "Hey, I can't play my sax tonight. I forgot my strap." But none of them was acceptable to me. I ended up fashioning a crude strap from some odds and ends I found backstage. While it wasn't nearly as comfortable as my real strap, it did the job. I had a stiff neck for the next couple of days but emerged unscathed otherwise.

Fostering Ownership in the Workplace

Accountable *leaders* are one thing, but what about accountable *team members*? All the same benefits apply. When team members believe in the value of *owning* the results of their behavior and decisions, leaders seldom have to *hold* them accountable. As former NBA player Joe Dumars once said, "On good teams, coaches hold players accountable. On great teams, players hold players accountable." If you've ever been on a team where this was true, you know how powerful mutually shared ownership is. I would argue that without it, a team will never reach its potential.

Make no mistake—building and sustaining an accountable workplace is not easy, especially when pointing fingers and placing blame are tolerated. So where to begin?

One of the most critical factors in establishing a culture of ownership is *psychological safety*: the belief that one will not be punished or humiliated for speaking up, asking questions, providing feedback, challenging ideas, or even making (honest) mistakes. Now may be a good time to assess the level of psychological safety on *your* team. It's virtually impossible to create a culture of ownership without it.

Good leaders are comfortable with opinions that don't match theirs, candid feedback that may sting, news that disappoints or frustrates, and questions that challenge the status quo. But great leaders go one step further, *encouraging* and *welcoming* alternative viewpoints that contradict their own.

Weak leaders, on the other hand, grow defensive. They adopt a "How dare you question ME?" attitude. They create workplaces where people fear expressing themselves freely. If you ever find yourself working for such a leader, my advice is: RUN! Misery is sure to follow. And if, after some self-reflection, you realize that *you* are such a leader, I strongly suggest you rethink your approach.

When it comes to the importance of ownership to a healthy culture, don't take my word for it. Research shows accountable organizations outperform unaccountable ones. Rather than point fingers, sweep problems under the rug, or waste time placing blame, accountable employees admit mistakes, take ownership for fixing them, and ensure they don't happen again. But they can only feel confident doing so in an environment hallmarked by psychological safety.

My workshop participants frequently mention *lack of accountable behavior* as their organization's biggest liability. Furthermore, research suggests members of Gen Z won't tolerate unaccountable behavior from their leaders. These young people are naturally skeptical of those in positions of power and, unlike previous generations, comfortable speaking up when something doesn't feel right. The Gen Zers I know personally are honest, opinionated, and unafraid to speak truth to power—one more reason to model ownership on your team.

By now, I hope it's clear that you won't sustain trust, loyalty, and engagement—everything you should want on your team—without *everyone* possessing a sense of ownership. So how can you as a leader cultivate a culture of ownership? Here are some ideas:

1. Set clear priorities, expectations, and goals. Misaligned expectations and ill-defined goals can reduce accountable behavior. For any task, job, project, or assignment you are requesting of someone, ensure you are crystal-clear in defining what you need or want. When priorities conflict, goals are ambiguous or constantly changing, or expectations are not clearly articulated, people become frustrated. Some will do the best they can under the circumstances while bitterly complaining. Others will "quiet quit"—they'll do the minimum and no more. Still others will throw up their hands altogether and blame coworkers for mistakes, missed deadlines, and sloppy work. To reduce uncertainty and drive accountability on your team, start by delineating the 5 W's succinctly and unambiguously:

- **Who** needs to be involved? **Who** will own the results? **Who** will benefit?
- **What** are the materials, resources, and/or supplies required to complete the task? **What** should the finished "product" look like and/or include?
- **When** is the deadline for the task to be completed?
- **Where** will the task be executed?
- **Why** is the task important?

Typically, the 5 W's are accompanied by an H—"How?" As a leader, you reserve the right to convey your expectations and goals regarding *how* a task should be accomplished. However, I find that the best leaders grant their people enough autonomy to figure out the *how* themselves. In other words, they identify the destination and leave it up to the employee to determine how to get there (while offering adequate resources, support, and encouragement along the way, of course). In her classic *Harvard Business Review* article "How to Kill Creativity," Teresa Amabile sums this idea up with an excellent analogy:

> When it comes to granting freedom, the key to creativity is giving people autonomy concerning the means—that is, concerning process—but not necessarily the ends. People will be more creative, in other words, if you give them

freedom to decide how to climb a particular mountain. You needn't let them choose which mountain to climb. In fact, clearly specified strategic goals often enhance people's creativity.

2. Lead by example. I recall a Nike TV commercial from the early '90s featuring former NBA player Charles Barkley. Under black-and-white footage of the grunting, perspiring superstar repeatedly dunking a basketball, Barkley intones: "I am not a role model. I'm not paid to be a role model. I'm paid to wreak havoc on the basketball court. Parents should be role models. Just because I dunk a basketball doesn't mean I should raise your kids."

While I admire Barkley's athleticism, he was wrong. Whether he saw himself as one or not, Barkley was definitely a role model. As a role model, I believe it was his obligation not simply to "wreak havoc on the basketball court" but to comport himself in a way befitting such an influential, high-profile athlete. Similarly, leaders are role models— whether they think they are or not. Being a role model just comes with the territory. Consequently, it's foolish to expect your people to act accountably if you don't. *Accountability begins with an organization's leaders.* It's simple: If you don't wish to be a role model, don't be a leader.

3. Provide sufficient resources. Failing to provide adequate resources to your people opens the door for unaccountable behavior to run rampant: "They didn't give me what I needed to do the job." Not giving adequate resources provides an easy justification for people to do the minimum or, in some cases, nothing at all. In *The Progress Principle*, Amabile and Kramer write: "Withholding necessary resources or rendering them difficult to access engenders a sense of futility, anger at having to waste time scrounging or doing 'grunt work,' and a perception that the project must not be very important." When that happens, blaming and finger-pointing are sure to follow.

4. Encourage open communication. I've already discussed the importance of clear, precise messaging, but it's worth revisiting here. Recall the "Draw a Bug" exercise from the chapter on Communication and how easy it is to misinterpret even simple instructions. When your communication lacks clarity, you pave the way for excuses that almost always include the phrase "I thought . . .":

- *"I thought* you needed that report by Friday. There's no way I can get it done by tomorrow."
- *"I thought* Jim was handling that."
- *"I thought* the meeting was canceled, so I made other plans."
- *"I thought* you just wanted a rough draft of the slide deck, not the final version."
- *"I thought* I had permission to make that decision, so I didn't ask anyone first."
- *"I thought* we had the budget for that, so I went ahead and submitted a purchase order."

While clear, precise communication won't solve *every* accountability issue on your team, it will go a long way toward reducing them.

5. Clarify consequences. When you were younger, you probably heard a lot of so-called "If/Then" statements—also known as *conditional statements*—from your parents or guardian(s). With a conditional statement, a "hypothesis" is presented in the first part, followed by a "conclusion" in the second part. How many of these sound familiar?

- If you finish your homework, you can go out and play.
- If you get good grades this semester, I'll get you a [fill in the blank] for your birthday.
- If you finish what's on your plate, you can have dessert.
- If you eat that entire sundae, you're going to get a stomachache.
- If you don't clean your room, you can forget about using the car this weekend.
- If you don't mow the lawn like I asked, you won't be seeing [boyfriend/girlfriend] any time soon.
- If you're not home by 9 p.m., it'll be the last time you go out unsupervised.

The power of these statements came from the unambiguous way they spelled out the *consequences* of your actions (or inactions). If you were an obedient kid, these If/Then statements helped keep you out of trouble and aided in your growth and development. (If you were a rebellious kid, well . . . that's a different story.)

In the workplace, conditional statements that clarify the consequences of a particular course of action (or inaction) can foster accountable behavior. By letting your people know the stakes involved with doing (or *not* doing) something, you underscore the urgency and importance of the task and increase the odds that it will be done right and on time.

6. Provide coaching. I'll have more to say about coaching later, but for now it's important to know its connection to accountability. Leaders who coach are in a prime position to offer employees constructive feedback and ensure they stay on track with assignments and projects. A trusted voice that tells people what they *need* to hear rather than what they *want* to hear will increase accountability for all who listen.

7. Create psychological safety around accountability. Creating the kind of work climate where people feel safe encourages them to take calculated risks (a hallmark of innovative companies) and come forward when mistakes are made or problems arise. Psychological safety is critical for success because it contributes to a workplace where employees invest their efforts in correcting problems rather than blaming each other. Leaders looking to develop psychological safety should encourage their people to raise issues, offer opposing points of view, or question decisions without fear of retribution (as long as it's done tactfully and respectfully). But be careful—if you don't "walk the talk" when it comes to psychological safety, you will rapidly lose trust and respect.

Grand Finale

Developing a sense of ownership among your team members doesn't just happen. A culture of ownership where people are accountable must be cultivated with intention and purpose. Like a composer continually modifying a piece of music, you may need to keep fine tuning until this note resounds within your team. I assure you that your efforts will be worth it.

Now It's Your Turn: Which of the ideas presented in this chapter are resonating most? Why?

You've read the chapter—now get the tool! Transform knowledge into action by downloading "Building a Sense of Ownership for Leader and Team Success" at

rightchordleadership.com/book-resources/

Note 4: Respect

Respect — treating others with dignity, valuing their opinions,
and validating their feelings — is a hallmark of effective leaders
and world-class organizations.

Conduct a Google search for "quotes on respect" and you'll end up with dozens of examples, including these:

- "We don't need to share the same opinions as others, but we need to be respectful." — Taylor Swift
- "I'm not concerned with your liking or disliking me. All I ask is that you respect me as a human being." — Jackie Robinson
- "I firmly believe that respect is a lot more important, and a lot greater, than popularity." — Julius Erving
- "We should all consider each other as human beings, and we should respect each other." — Malala Yousafzai

While these quotes are inspiring, they assume we *already* know what respect is. Sure, we *should* respect others — but what exactly does that mean?

The Oxford dictionary defines the *noun* respect as "a feeling of deep admiration for someone or something elicited by their abilities, qualities, or achievements." Similarly, it defines the *verb* respect as "admire (someone or something) deeply, as a result of their abilities, qualities, or achievements." These definitions are fine, but for me "admire" doesn't quite capture the *essence* of what respect is all about.

I define respect as acknowledging and honoring someone's inherent worth, value, or importance through your words and actions. There are hundreds of ways to do this. Here are just a few:

- Recognize the validity of another's perspective, even if you disagree
- Listen closely without interrupting when others speak
- Show consideration for others' personal space and boundaries
- Solicit another's opinion on an important matter
- Be on time for meetings and appointments
- Show appreciation for the efforts and sacrifices of others
- Anticipate and fulfill another's needs
- Respond to inquiries in a timely fashion

This is a short list, of course. But even a few examples are sufficient to demonstrate that showing respect for others doesn't require much effort. In most instances, a little courtesy, thoughtfulness, or consideration is enough. But if you want to really amp up your respect game, take special note of that last bullet point. I don't know when "ghosting" became all the rage, but it is rampant these days—especially when it comes to responding to emails. While I'm not suggesting you reply to every spam email or solicitation you receive from a stranger, if the sender's request seems legitimate, I strongly recommend responding in some fashion. Even a "no thanks" is preferable to no response at all. For people you know, a reply of some kind is mandatory in my opinion—even if it's to decline an invitation or offer. For example, I recently asked an attendee at one of my workshops to write me a testimonial on LinkedIn. In my request, I stated that if he would rather not, it was perfectly fine. He responded: "Mike, you're great and I'm going to pass. Thanks, and take care." Although he declined, I was impressed he took the time to write back. I've lost track of the number of clients, students, and business prospects who express gratitude when they receive a reply from me within a few hours. Prompt replies are small gestures of respect that go a long way. So leave the "ghosting" for Halloween.

Respect is the adhesive that holds great teams and organizations together. Without it, everything breaks down like an engine running on old, dirty motor oil. In fact, a 2021 study in *MIT Sloan Management Review* found that the most crucial factor in a positive employee experience is leaders, managers, and peers treating employees with respect. According to the study, "the single best predictor of a company's culture score is whether employees feel respected at work. *Respect is not only the most important factor; it stands head and shoulders above other cultural elements in terms of its importance* [italics added]."

Conflict and Respect

The way you address conflict reflects the amount of respect you have for others. Let's do a quick thought experiment. Close your eyes and take a moment to imagine how it *feels* to be in a conflict. You may want to recall a specific conflict or just think about conflict more generally. The important thing is to recollect the *feeling* of being in conflict. What words and images come to mind? Jot them down now.

If violent words and imagery popped into your head just now, you're not alone. I've asked hundreds of workshop participants to do this exercise, then had them translate their feelings into words and images on a piece of paper. Almost all of them draw negative images and use negative language, such as angry faces, rainclouds, tanks, cannons, lightning bolts, car crashes, and profanity. My favorite drawing ever was of two crudely drawn stick figures, one with an ax embedded in its skull. A fountain of blood, depicted with a dark red crayon, spurted from a gaping head wound. I asked the audience who drew the picture and a woman in the back of the room claimed ownership. I asked her what the gruesome image represented.

"That's me and my husband!" she replied without hesitation.

Everyone, including me, howled with laughter (although, admittedly, a part of me was concerned for her spouse's safety).

Such frightening art used to surprise me, but no longer. Conflict can certainly be — and often is — toxic and vindictive. We've all experienced conflict that leaves us feeling resentful, bitter, or enraged. No wonder so many of my workshop participants resort to highly charged words and images in that exercise.

Now consider this: How might your response to conflict be affected if you typically think about it this way? Wouldn't you automatically enter conflicts ready for a fight? You'd likely view conflict as a brawl of sorts where there can be only one winner and one loser. And you'd be prepared to do almost *anything* to emerge victorious. Of course, the other person — your foe, if you will — would think the same about *you*.

This "all or nothing" situation is known as a "zero-sum game," a term borrowed from game theory. With a zero-sum game, any gain by one party *must* come at the expense of the other party. In other words, one person's advantage becomes another's disadvantage. Sporting events are typically zero-sum. Unless the rules of a sport allow for a tie, there is always one winner and one loser (or one first place, one second place, etc.).

You may have grown up in a home where conflict was viewed this way. And while there are times when "playing for all the marbles" is appropriate, this is typically *not* the best way to handle conflict in the workplace. That's why the first step in managing conflict effectively is to *change your attitude toward it*. Once you are open to the idea that *conflict can be healthy and constructive*, you've taken the first step toward building more respectful relationships with the people in your life.

The fact is, whether conflict is ultimately *constructive* or *destructive* largely depends on how well you *manage* it. Conflict is *destructive* when it

- Undermines trust and morale,
- Polarizes people and groups,
- Increases or sharpens differences, and
- Leads to irresponsible and harmful behavior, such as harassment or fighting.

On the other hand, conflict is *constructive* when it

- Allows for the airing of different ideas and worldviews,
- Helps move the organization toward its goals,

- Increases productivity rather than hampers it,
- Results in clarification of issues, and
- Leads to people learning about each other.

ACES

Too often we allow conflict to drive a wedge between us and the other person. Convinced we're right, we stick to *our* opinion while the other party sticks to *their* opinion (again, recall the ingenious cartoon with the two characters disputing whether the number is a 6 or a 9). Back and forth we go, generating a lot of heat but not much light. The good news is: if you want better outcomes, there's an easy-to-remember method that can help. It's called **ACES — A, C, E, S.** ACES stands for

- **A**cknowledge the problem,
- **C**ontrol your emotions,
- **E**ncourage dialogue, and
- **S**tate next steps.

If you follow the ACES approach the next time you're embroiled in a conflict, you'll improve your chances of achieving a mutually beneficial resolution. Let's briefly discuss each letter before conducting a more in-depth examination:

Acknowledge the problem. A scene in the legendary film *Jaws* features Chief Brody (played by Roy Scheider) begrudgingly shoveling "chum" — bloody fish parts — from a boat to attract the shark that's been terrorizing his beach community. Suddenly, the massive fish breaches, baring its massive, razor-sharp teeth and revealing itself in plain view for the first time. A stunned Brody slowly backs into the boat's wheelhouse where shark hunter Quint (played by Robert Shaw) is stationed.

"You're gonna need a bigger boat," Brody says quietly (a line that was apparently improvised).

Talk about acknowledging the problem! When we pretend a problem or conflict doesn't exist — or hope it will resolve itself if we simply ignore it — the situation *almost always* gets worse. It may take courage to acknowledge a problem exists, but it's the vital first step toward eventual resolution.

Control your emotions. Earlier, I explained that self-management, your ability to control your emotions, is a key dimension of emotional intelligence. When you're in a conflict, controlling your emotions is a sign of respect. Think of the times you've witnessed somebody lose their cool — if you were on the receiving end of that spectacle, would you respect that individual? I doubt it. This is not to say you can't have a strong opinion about something. But whenever I observe someone throwing a temper tantrum, I immediately lose respect for them. Infants throw tantrums; adults should know better.

I realize it may be difficult at times to keep your emotions in check, especially if the other person is being inflexible or has a point of view that strongly contradicts yours. But leadership isn't about doing what's easy. It's about doing what's *right* – for you, your team, and your organization.

Encourage dialogue. A recent *Reader's Digest* article titled "Why Do Adult Siblings Stop Speaking? The Psychology Behind Family Estrangement and Sibling Rivalries" includes sad stories of siblings who don't speak for decades. I can't help but think what could have been had one of the siblings summoned the courage to initiate dialogue. Without dialogue, resentment can fester for weeks, months, years, even decades. As a leader, you demonstrate respect for the other person by (1) effectively managing the emotions you may be experiencing and (2) opening the door to a conversation.

State next steps. It's a mistake to leave a conversation without identifying next steps. Next steps could take the form of:

- A follow-up conversation
- More frequent check-ins (verbal or written)
- A particular action or activity
- A change in a process or procedure

Remember that clarity of communication is key here. Expectations regarding next steps should be spelled out plainly, thereby limiting the possibility of excuses should they not be met.

Let's examine each step in more depth.

Acknowledge the Problem

When you're facing a conflict, acknowledging there's a problem may seem obvious. What sense would it make *not* to acknowledge it? It turns out there are many reasons why admitting a problem exists can be difficult:

- **Problems require time and energy to solve.** It's easier to ignore a problem in the hope that it will just go away. This tactic rarely works, of course. In fact, it usually makes matters worse.
- **We think it may make us look bad.** When a problem arises, we may fear others will assume we're not competent, or that we're unable to lead effectively. Consequently, we downplay the problem or tell people we're handling it when we're actually denying or avoiding it.
- **We may need to engage in uncomfortable conversations.** Many of us know from experience that difficult conversations can lead to hurt feelings, raised voices, tears, nasty accusations, or worse. The prospect of holding such a conversation can fill our brains with negativity — and who wants to deal with all that messy stuff if they don't have to? Better to say and do nothing, right?

While at least some anxiety is understandable, *none of these excuses will bring you closer to a desirable resolution.* That's why the first step in solving any conflict is recognizing there's a problem. As a wise person once said, "Avoidance is the best short-term strategy to escape conflict, and the best long-term strategy to ensure suffering."

Whose suffering?

Yours, mostly.

I recommend these three steps (the "Three A's") for acknowledging a problem to my clients:

1. Aim for Authenticity
2. Anticipate Resistance
3. Adjust Your Attitude

The First A: Aim for Authenticity. In their best-selling book *Crucial Conversations*, authors Kerry Patterson, Joseph Grenny, Ron McMillan, and Al Switzler assert that whether or not a conflict is successfully resolved largely depends on what we do *before* we open our mouths. I agree 100 percent. Prior to initiating the conversation, consider your *intent*: Is your intent to make yourself feel superior or demonstrate why the other person is wrong? Or is it to try to satisfy (as much as possible) the needs of all parties? The first approach is unlikely to yield the best outcome, while the second approach has a much greater chance of succeeding. Reflecting on our intent *before* speaking forces us to slow down and *think* rather than react impulsively.

Imagine you're upset at a coworker, Jen, whom you believe is not doing her share of the work. Irritated by her inaction, you decide to speak to her. Here is what your inner narrative might sound like:

> I need to speak with Jen about this issue that's bugging me, but I don't want to come off as attacking or disrespecting her. I want to express my feelings, but I also want Jen to believe that I've listened to her side of the story with patience and empathy. I'm not looking to be best friends, but I would like us to remain cordial and professional. After all, we have to work together. So, what chords must I play to achieve these objectives?

Can you see how this exercise applies the brakes to our impetuous, emotion-fueled "runaway train" brain ("I'm going to give her a piece of my mind!") and creates a more thoughtful, less antagonistic mindset?

When you speak with Jen, you should continue to aim for authenticity. You may want to consider the following "opening chords" (feel free to modify the wording to fit your situation):

- "I'd like to talk with you about how we work together and get your perspective/thoughts on the best way to do that. Can we find a time to sit down and discuss it?"
- "I'd like to better understand your work schedule so that we can potentially get things done more efficiently. Can we chat about it and see if we can find common ground?"
- "My goal in wanting to talk with you is to discuss how to optimize our working relationship in a way that feels good for both of us. How do you feel about discussing it?"

As the conversation proceeds, you may want to interject something like this (again, feel free to modify the wording to fit your situation):

- "I think we need to come up with a solution for how we can best work together going forward. Can we brainstorm some ideas?"
- "Let's work together to find a way to resolve [issue] in a way that works for both of us."

- "It's important to me to find a way to improve our [relationship/work/understanding]. What are your thoughts?"

Notice each of the items above is purposely designed to mitigate a defensive reaction. Not one is accusatory, critical, or confrontational. When you come out of the gate with negative body language, tone, and language, the other person will instantly put up their defenses. On the other hand, when you adopt a neutral tone and a problem-solving orientation, you are far more likely to have a fruitful conversation. Aiming for authenticity also yields the best results when you need to be more direct and assertive with an employee. Consider these examples:

- "I have some concerns about [issue] that I'd like to discuss with you."
- "I've noticed that [specific behavior] has been affecting your work, and I'd like to discuss how we can address it."
- "I realize this isn't an easy conversation, but I believe it's necessary for us to have an honest discussion about [issue]."

While these statements are more straightforward than the previous ones, they are still authentic, truthful, and signaling positive intent. They show that you can be both authentic *and* direct without being a jerk.

The Second A: Anticipate Resistance. When you anticipate resistance, you stay alert to what the other person does or says. Are they about to explode with anger? Start crying? Shut down completely? Blame someone else? Like a world-class chess player, you need to be ready with an effective move no matter what the other person does. Use the formula "If he/she does X, I will do Y." Keep your antenna up and be ready to pivot, if necessary.

For example, let's say that during your conversation with Jen, she states, "To be honest, I don't know why you're coming down on me like this. I do my fair share of work just like everyone else."

To extend the chess metaphor, she just put you in check. Your next move is critical. Fortunately, you anticipated this sort of deflection might be her defense—and you're ready for it.

"It's not my intent to 'come down' on you, and I apologize if it feels that way. It's just that I've noticed some deadlines have been missed and that you've been leaving early and relying on the rest of the team to finish up."

"I left early the other day because I had a family commitment. Sorry about that. But missed deadlines? I don't think so."

Check.

"Actually, you left at least a half hour early *three times* last week—Tuesday, Wednesday, and Thursday. I only know this because I came by all three times to ask you a question and you weren't at your desk. And both the sales report *and* job log for this week are overdue. If they're completed, I haven't seen them."

Jen, faced with facts, offers up some excuses for her behavior. You're in control now.

"Look, Jen, I don't mind if you have to leave early on occasion. We all do. What I would ask, though, is that you let me know first rather than just leaving. That way, the team and I can be best prepared. And it's critical you meet those deadlines. Otherwise, it throws off our weekly schedule and makes more work for all of us. I know there's a lot on your plate right now. If you need assistance, please let me know and we'll talk through it. How does that sound?"

By anticipating resistance and addressing it with tact and composure, you're more likely to have a positive conversation. Of course, your conversations are likely to be more complex than the hypothetical one above, but the fundamentals remain the same:

- Focus on specific behaviors and incidents, not personality
- Use facts in making your case, not speculation
- Avoid attacking the other person
- Encourage collaborative problem-solving
- Offer support

The Third A: Adjust Your Attitude. You should make an agreement with yourself to remain diplomatic throughout your interaction. Belligerence or combativeness won't help you achieve your objective of a mutually agreeable resolution. Even if the other person is rude or curt, *you* play the right chords and set the example.

Adjusting our attitude can become more difficult the more we feel ourselves getting worked up. Our emotions have to be kept in check, especially if the other party's aren't, or the conversation will quickly spiral out of control. That leads us right into the next step of the ACES model.

Control Your Emotions

Recently, one of my coaching clients (I'll call her Beth) told me about a difficult colleague at her place of employment (I'll call her Susan). Beth and Susan had been butting heads for a while. Finally, Beth decided to approach Susan to try to clear the air. Susan agreed to speak with Beth but began the encounter by asking in a terse tone, "So what exactly is your goal for this meeting?"

Beth told me she was initially caught off guard but quickly recovered. Beth calmly explained that she hoped to clarify some possible misconceptions and see how the two could work together more effectively. According to Beth, by the end of the conversation, Susan was less hostile and more receptive. I attribute Susan's change in attitude to Beth's nonconfrontational reaction, as well as her unwillingness to respond in kind (what I call "taking the bait").

Of course, controlling emotions under stress can be challenging. This has less to do with our personality or character than with our physiology—specifically, the way our brains are wired. Remember when we discussed self-management earlier and how the amygdala is like the body's smoke detector? Several physiological changes occur when the amygdala is on high alert: heartbeat quickens, blood pressure rises, breathing shortens, and so on. We may even become disoriented or feel our heads getting fuzzy or foggy. In addition, so-called stress hormones are released, preparing our bodies for an emergency response. When our brains and bodies are in this revved-up state, our ability to think rationally becomes significantly impaired, and we're more likely to lash out physically, verbally, or both.

We can't change the way our brains are hardwired, but we can tone down our reactions with self-awareness and discipline. As I suggested earlier, the key is to intentionally and purposefully *choose* our response to conflict—not to react impulsively and succumb to fight or flight. When we *choose* empathy over personal attacks and joint problem-solving over accusations and assumptions, we set the table for the discovery of mutually agreeable resolutions.

One of the most valuable tools for achieving this outcome is the "pause button." Pushing the pause button—that is, taking a few moments to *think* before responding—is not easy, especially when emotions are boiling over and our "smoke alarms" are going crazy. How many times have you said something unkind during a disagreement you wish you could take back? How many times have you tried to refrain from uttering a snarky retort, only to hear yourself saying it anyway? If this has happened to you, don't worry. Today is a new day, and there's never been a better time to start practicing pushing the pause button during a conflict.

Let's look at a process that can help. The following suggestions about mindfulness, excerpted from a *Harvard Business Review* article titled "Calming Your Brain During Conflict" by Diane Musho Hamilton, are designed to tamp down your emotions so you can choose a more constructive response. If you follow this advice, you'll gain control over your emotions rather than allow them to gain control over you.

According to Hamilton, the first step in practicing mindfulness when triggered is to notice we've been provoked. We may perceive a shift in our tone of voice, gripping sensations in our belly, or a sudden desire to retreat. Rather than ignore or dismiss these sensations, Hamilton asserts, we must be present, curious, and willing to explore the experience rather than run from it.

Letting go of the story is the next step. Hamilton writes: "We need to completely let go of the judging mind. This is a very challenging step because when we feel threatened, the mind immediately fills with all kinds of difficult thoughts and stories about what's happening." It's true. When we're upset, we tell ourselves stories about people's motivations and intentions that are often inaccurate. These stories can be difficult to dismiss because we tend to believe evidence that supports them and reject evidence that doesn't. However, staying receptive to possibilities *other than* the story we've created can slow down our hare brain and allow our tortoise brain to catch up.

Hamilton also suggests that breathing is important. She recommends breathing rhythmically, for example, counting "one . . . two . . . three . . . four" as you *inhale* and "one . . . two . . . three . . . four . . . five . . . six" as you *exhale*, then repeating the count several times. Your breath should be even and smooth, and the volume of breath should stay consistent. Hamilton says paying attention to our body reestablishes equilibrium, restoring our ability to think, listen, and relate.

We've already discussed that responding to volume with volume and aggression with aggression is not typically helpful.

So, what should you do when *someone else's* emotions are out of control? When the emotion *behind* the message overwhelms the message itself, you need to defuse it *before* tackling the message. Not doing so can lead to a rapidly escalating confrontation. Remember those rams butting heads from earlier? Someone pass the Advil!

Encourage Dialogue

The ability to initiate and sustain productive dialogue when in conflict is not a skill we're born with. It must be learned, practiced, and honed over time. Here are some suggestions to help you develop aptitude in this area:

Avoid using absolutes such as "you always" or "you never." These are likely to trigger a defensive reaction from the other person. Why? Because it's hardly ever the case that someone *always* or *never* does something. As soon as a person hears "You always" or "You never," they'll feel compelled to share a long list of examples contradicting your claim. Avoid going down that path by preparing *specific examples* of undesirable behavior. For example, "For the past three days I've noticed you . . ." or "At the last meeting, I heard you say . . ." While the other person may still push back on your examples, it's much harder than contesting vague generalities.

Don't act dismissively or condescendingly. While the other person's issue or problem may not mean much to you, it does to them. It's fine to *disagree* with their point of view (as long as you explain why) but invalidating or discrediting their concern will increase the likelihood of a defensive response. Avoid sarcasm for the same reason. You may think you're being funny or clever, but when emotions are churning and rational thought is compromised, sarcasm is counterproductive.

Watch your body language. Your words may sound genuine, but your body language can communicate something else entirely. Rolling eyes, crossed arms, and pursed lips signal annoyance. Stay attuned to what your face and body are doing as you speak. If your body language tends to "give away" what you're feeling, you may need to practice keeping it in check.

Offer affirmations as you conclude. Remember how small wins can have significant inner work life benefits? If we want what we say to stick, we don't want to leave the other person feeling dejected. We should demonstrate that the effort they are putting in is appreciated, and affirmations can go a long way in doing that. Take a look at these examples of affirmation:

- I know this conversation wasn't easy. I appreciate your honesty and willingness to improve.
- It was helpful to learn more about your situation. I think we made some real progress.
- Thank you for being open to my suggestions today. I value our relationship.

These end the conversation on a positive, optimistic note.

State Next Steps

This is the final stage of the ACES model. Once a resolution has been reached, don't assume the other person fully understands what it entails. Ensure that whatever resolution you decide on is clear and unambiguous. Remember from earlier that what seems obvious to you may not to the other person— even if they insist it is. You can increase the clarity of any next steps by asking four simple questions:

1. Who?
2. What?
3. When?
4. How?

More specifically, the questions work together like this:

WHO . . . will do **WHAT** . . . by **WHEN** . . . And **HOW** will we follow up?

For example, let's say you and a colleague named Rob have resolved a conflict around his ongoing lateness. You acknowledged there was a problem, initiated a conversation, controlled your emotions, deftly managed Rob's emotions, and landed on a path forward. Now it's time to clarify next steps. Your portion of the exchange might go like this:

"Before we conclude, let's quickly review where things stand. You committed to being on time starting tomorrow and to call me if you're going to be late in the future. We'll meet on the 15th of next month to see if any issues still exist and discuss how your commute is going. How does that sound?"

Notice all four questions have been addressed: *Your employee* (WHO) committed to being *on time* (WHAT) starting *tomorrow* (WHEN) and to call if they're going to be late in the future. You'll *meet on the 15th of next month* (WHEN) to see if any issues still exist and discuss how their commute is going (HOW).

It's a sign of respect to give the other person a chance to confirm next steps or amend them, if necessary. If your colleague continues to be late, however, you can refer to your conversation and the agreement you made. The who/what/when/how questions build accountability into your conversation and give you, as the leader, a set of clear commitments to lean on if needed in the future.

Grand Finale

Picture this: The members of Flip Like Wilson, the band I helped found in 1995, arrive at a gig sometime in the late '90s. We ascend a flight of stairs to the dressing room and, upon entering, behold a scene reminiscent of an all-night celebration (minus the passed-out people, thankfully). Open containers of Chinese food lie on their sides, their contents spilling out onto the floor. Plates of half-eaten shrimp lo mein and kung pao chicken are scattered about the room along with crumpled napkins and used plastic silverware. Empty beer bottles are everywhere. It looks like a marauding horde of amped-up partygoers just blew through, leaving a chaotic mess in their wake.

Our manager, the room's only other occupant, greets us. "Are you hungry?" he asks. "Help yourself if you want."

I remember surveying the spectacle with a mixture of revulsion and astonishment. Was he serious? Did he not understand how disrespectful it was to invite us to partake of another band's cold leftovers? A heartfelt apology for the clutter, rather than an invitation to dine, would have been more appropriate.

To be clear, we were never a band that expected, let alone insisted on, food at our shows. If food was offered, we were always grateful. But this — this was insulting. The message we received was that we weren't worthy of our own meal, that picked-over scraps were perfectly acceptable. We took the incident in stride and didn't make a fuss, choosing instead to politely decline. To this day, we still joke about it (although it wasn't funny at the time) and the impression it made. Some moments of disrespect, it turns out, are hard to let go of, even decades later.

Of course, nobody is obligated to respect everyone they meet. But if you want to lead effectively, you'll need to consistently demonstrate respect for individuals in word and deed — including those with whom you disagree or don't particularly like. It's part of the job of leadership. As former Philadelphia mayor Michael Nutter said, "You get respect when you give respect. *That's* how you get respect."

Now It's Your Turn: Which of the ideas presented in this chapter are resonating most? Why?

You've read the chapter — now get the tool! Enhance your learning experience by downloading "Fostering Respect: Where Do You Stand?" at

rightchordleadership.com/book-resources/

Note 5: Direction

Setting a clear direction with a bold organizational vision serves as a "North Star" whose guidance focuses, energizes, and unifies people.

In a 2020 Medium article titled "Kid A: A Love Letter to Radiohead's Masterpiece," author Shawn Eastridge reflects on the album's 20th anniversary with the following insight:

> While I love nearly everything they've produced, *Kid A* stands alone as a singular work beamed fully-formed from outer space or some other plane of existence. When it was released on October 2, 2000, many fans and critics expected Radiohead to follow U2's trajectory, expanding their sound and opting for more bombast that would fit right in at the larger venues they'd been playing. Instead, driven by [lead singer] Thom Yorke's near-debilitating mental breakdowns and depression, Radiohead sped full-force in the opposite direction.
>
> The group abandoned nearly every trend, technique and gimmick they'd perfected over the course of the 90s, opting instead for disconnected electronics and nightmarish soundscapes which reflected the paranoia, disconnect and outright panic of an ever-evolving digital landscape and the dawn of the new millennium. *Kid A* transcended all the standard pop music trappings, offering listeners a direct tunnel into the void from which it emerged. It is a vision of the end, a terrifying dream, a desperate cry for help and, above all, a remarkable artistic achievement.

What Eastridge describes so eloquently here is, simply put, Radiohead's *direction* circa 2000 (he even uses the word). Emerging from the commercial and critical success of predecessor *OK Computer*, band members proffered various ideas for the next record. Guitarist Ed O'Brien, for example, pushed for a more straight-ahead rock album. But singer Thom Yorke resisted, telling a magazine: "There was no chance of the album sounding like that. I'd completely had it with melody. I just wanted rhythm. All melodies to me were pure embarrassment." As the other band members struggled to get on the same creative page with Yorke, with some even considering quitting, Yorke forged ahead with his concept—an album that drew influences from a multitude of unorthodox musical styles, employed unusual instrumentation, and eschewed conventional song structure. At the time, O'Brien lamented, "It's scary—everyone feels insecure. I'm a guitarist and suddenly it's like, well, there are no guitars on this track, or no drums."

It was a risk, sure, but the risk paid off—*Kid A* debuted at number one on the UK Albums Chart and became the band's first number one album on the US Billboard 200. It sold remarkably well in many countries around the globe and was even nominated for the Grammy Award for Album of the Year.

Simply put, Radiohead's direction at the time was "away from whatever had worked previously." But it was more than that. A deliberate rebuke of the impressive achievements they'd enjoyed up to that point, *Kid A* announced a bold new Radiohead unafraid to shake things up. The direction they chose was fraught with peril, perhaps—but it was a direction nonetheless. With conviction and confidence, they followed their instincts to a destination that proved artistically rewarding for themselves as well as their millions of fans.

The Irish rock band U2 experienced a similar reinvention in the late '80s, after the release of the album *Rattle and Hum* in 1988. Although *Rattle and Hum*—an album seeped in American blues, folk, and gospel music—sold well, critics lambasted it as bombastic and pretentious. Like Radiohead after them, U2 set forth in a new musical direction. Inspired by musical styles that had become popular at that time—alternative rock, industrial music, and electronic dance music, primarily—the band abandoned the earnest rock anthems of 1987's *The Joshua Tree* and *Rattle and Hum*'s blues-based elements for a darker, more inward-looking approach. Just as with Radiohead, the recording sessions were contentious as band members bickered over their new direction and songwriting. There was even talk of disbanding (no pun intended)—hardly surprising considering coproducer Brian Eno felt his role was "to come in and erase anything that sounded too much like U2."

Rather than break up, however, U2 produced one of their most acclaimed and beloved albums, *Achtung Baby*. Released in 1991, it debuted at number one on the US Billboard 200 Top Albums and appeared at the top of sales charts around the world. The album produced five successful singles, sold 18 million copies worldwide, and won a Grammy for Best Rock Performance by a Duo or Group with Vocal.

Like Radiohead and U2, leaders who articulate a strong *direction* for their team stimulate a sense of propulsive movement that focuses, aligns, and energizes people. In this context, "direction" is not a synonym for "instruction" (i.e., how to do something). As the fifth note of the CHORDS Model, it refers to carving a clear and audacious path toward a compelling future state that members of a team or organization navigate together. A direction to which all team members commit transcends the routine tasks and duties of the average workday, galvanizing collaboration and imbuing work with meaning beyond merely earning a paycheck.

What Is a Vision?

Establishing a direction starts by formulating a bold organizational or team *vision*. In short, a vision is typically a short statement (or series of statements) that defines *who* you *want* to be collectively and *why*. (This is different from a team or organizational mission that defines your *purpose*, i.e., what you do.) The most memorable visions I've come across are expressions of an optimal future state to which an organization or team aspires. It may be helpful to think of a vision as a "North Star" whose steadfast guidance focuses and unites people in achieving ambitious goals. The best visions are aspirational yet succinct; they paint a compelling picture of a desirable destination, one that influences every interaction and inspires people to endeavor for something greater every day.

As a professional jazz musician, I've always been intrigued by the notion of artistic visions. Indeed, developing a unique artistic vision is one of the most challenging aspects of learning to play jazz. Just as an artistic vision is critical to jazz musicians, having a team or organizational vision is critical to business leaders. Compelling visions tap into our innate need to aspire, to seek something greater than what we are today. The word "aspire" has roots in Old French (*aspirer*) or classical Latin (*aspirare*), meaning "to breathe." In a beautifully poetic sense, then, pursuing a vision is akin to breathing and should be similarly invigorating and revitalizing rather than a chore. When an organizational vision is magnified through the collective actions of a harmonious workforce, the results can be astounding.

You can often get a sense of a company's vision after spending a short amount of time there. Several years ago, for example, I led a workshop at Maliban, one of Sri Lanka's largest biscuit manufacturers. As I waited in the lobby, I couldn't help but notice the energy in the place. Employees greeted me with a friendly "Good morning!" as they passed. TV screens played Maliban commercials filled with colorful images and catchy songs. Awards and trophies lined numerous glass cases. I wasn't surprised to learn later that Maliban's vision is "To be the most successful and respected food company in Sri Lanka." I'm not suggesting the company's vision was solely responsible for the energy and enthusiasm I observed, but I'm confident it played an outsized role.

In his classic article "What Leaders Really Do," first published in 1990, John P. Kotter makes a provocative point about visions:

Most discussions of vision have a tendency to degenerate into the mystical. The implication is that a vision is something mysterious that mere mortals, even talented ones, could never hope to have. But developing good business direction isn't magic. It is a tough, sometimes exhausting process of gathering and analyzing information. People who articulate such visions aren't magicians but broad-based strategic thinkers who are willing to take risks.

I can't think of any high-performing individual, team, or organization that doesn't have a bold vision driving the pursuit of excellence. Take the legendary Miles Davis album *Kind of Blue*, one of the highest-selling jazz albums of all time. Of the album, Miles himself said, "I didn't write out the music for *Kind of Blue*, but brought in sketches for what everybody was supposed to play because *I wanted a lot of spontaneity in the playing* [italics added]."

Miles's quote reflects the audacious vision the iconic trumpeter had for his art: the desire for maximum freedom in the music. Without Miles's keen vision, *Kind of Blue* would have been a good album but likely not a masterpiece.

Another of my favorite examples of a bold vision concerns the rock band Queen and their hit "Bohemian Rhapsody." According to a 1976 Rolling Stone article titled "Queen: Four Queens Beat Opera Flush" (quoted on the webpage *Queen Archives*), lead singer Freddie Mercury said of the much-loved song, "I always wanted to do something operatic. I wanted something with a mood setter at the start, going into a rock type of thing which completely breaks off into an opera section, a vicious twist and then returns to the theme. I don't really know anything about opera myself. Just certain pieces. I wanted to create what I thought Queen could do. It's not authentic . . . certainly not. It's no sort of pinch out of [the Mozart opera] *Magic Flute*. It was as far as my limited capacity could take me."

Mercury's vision for a rock opera is certainly admirable. But his tenacity in the face of criticism is even more so. For example, did you know:

- Record executives told him that "Bohemian Rhapsody" would never be a hit?
- Other musicians insisted it would never be played on the radio?
- Critics called it "a superficially impressive pastiche of incongruous musical styles" with "no immediate selling point whatsoever" and "scarcely a shred of a tune among its many parts"?

Mercury may have had his doubters, but his innovative vision helped birth one of the most recognized and beloved rock songs ever recorded.

Do you have a bold vision for your team that falls outside familiar norms? Good. If enough people push back, you're probably on to something.

As the late composer and music theorist John Cage said, "I can't understand why people are frightened of new ideas. I'm frightened of the old ones."

When my band Flip Like Wilson was founded in 1995, we cultivated a bold yet simple vision for ourselves: *to be the best cover band on the Philadelphia/New Jersey/Delaware music scene.* We didn't want to be a conventional band that played all the expected hits. Sure, the usual suspects showed up occasionally (I'm looking at *you*, "Livin' on a Prayer") but most of the songs in our repertoire were unconventional selections.

At the height of the alternative music scene in the mid-'90s, this proved to be a successful formula. We quickly garnered a large and devoted following by (1) NOT playing typical cover band songs, (2) including songs by rap artists such as A Tribe Called Quest, Beastie Boys, and Run DMC, and (3) rotating singers to keep things interesting for the audience. Within a few years, we were setting attendance records at venues up and down the East Coast. We continue to perform today, 30 years after our first gig!

Without a clearly defined sense of direction, we wouldn't have been nearly as successful right out of the gate—and we certainly wouldn't be playing today. The musical vision we developed at the band's inception was the engine that compelled us to keep pushing the boundaries of what a cover band could . . . well, cover. We knew that if *everyone* on the team drove toward the *same* destination with enthusiasm, energy, and a "take no prisoners" attitude, anything was possible.

How about one more example, this time a business one? In a YouTube video I frequently share with clients, Steve Jobs is shown at Apple's Worldwide Developer Conference in 1997. He'd just returned to Apple as an advisor after getting fired 12 years earlier. In the video, Jobs invites an audience member standing at a mic to ask him a question. The man says, "It's sad and clear that on several counts you've discussed, you don't know what you're talking about. I would like, for example, for you to express in clear terms how, say, Java and any of its incarnations addresses the ideas embodied in OpenDoc. And when you're finished with that, perhaps you can tell us what you personally have been doing for the last seven years."

The crowd goes silent. Another attendee can be heard saying "Ouch."

Ouch, indeed.

Not only is Jobs's response a masterclass in keeping your cool in a strained situation, but he outlines a clear, unambiguous vision for Apple that has since become a company hallmark. I'll share a few highlights from his response because it provides such a powerful lesson in cultivating and communicating an audacious organizational vision (not to mention a lesson in how to lower the temperature during a tense exchange):

> One of the hardest things when you're trying to effect change is that people like this gentleman are right in some areas. . . . The hardest thing is: how does that fit in to a cohesive, larger vision that's going to allow you to sell 8 billion dollars, 10 billion dollars of product a year? And one of the things I've always found is that you've got to start with the customer experience and work backwards to the technology. You can't start with the technology and try to figure out where you're going to try to sell it. And I've made this mistake probably more than anybody else in this room. And I got the scar tissue to prove it. And I know that it's the case.
>
> And as we have tried to come up with a strategy and a vision for Apple, it started with "What incredible benefits can we give to the customer? Where can we take the customer?" Not starting with "Let's sit down with the engineers and figure out what awesome technology we have and then how are we going to market that?" And I think that's the right path to take. . . . Some mistakes will be made, by the way. Some mistakes will be made along the way. That's good because at least some decisions are being made along the way. And we'll find the mistakes and we'll fix them.
>
> Some people will be pissed off, some people will not know what they're talking about, but I think it is so much better than where things were not very long ago. And I think we're going to get there.

Jobs's vision for Apple is succinct yet compelling and inspiring. It's a brilliantly articulated nugget of future-focused ambition that not only skillfully answers his critic but defines the road map Apple will take to become one of the most successful companies in the world.

While a well-articulated vision can inspire effort and enthusiasm, an ill-defined one—or the lack of one altogether— can cause people to disengage and become apathetic. In her 2021 online *Harvard Business Review* article "5 Reasons Your Employees Don't Understand Your Company's Vision," author Sabina Nawaz offers the following pitfalls for leaders to consider when creating and conveying a vision:

1. **Lack of communication.** A single mention at a meeting or in an email is insufficient for people to truly "get" your vision. Good leaders reinforce the company or team vision often by sharing recent success stories that reflect it. For example, let's say your vision as the supervisor of a call center is to be "the most responsive, efficient, customer-centric call center in the northeast region." Every month, you might spotlight employees who demonstrate extraordinary customer service regardless of the size and dollar value of the account. If you consistently look for ways to bring the vision alive and make it real for people, they will begin to see it as more than just words.

2. **Different altitudes.** You read that right: *altitudes*, not attitudes. There is a tendency for vision statements to be grand, lofty expressions with little connection to the actual work people do in the organization. This is a

sure recipe for failure. According to Nawaz, "[Visions] might sound good but leave too much to the imagination of an employee operating lower to the ground, trying to make a connection between their day job and the purported purpose of the organization." People shouldn't have to work hard to "connect the dots" between the team or organizational vision and their own work. Part of your job as a leader is to ensure a "clear line of sight" between the organizational or team vision and your employees' contributions. For example, I recently helped a client craft a vision that honored their family roots as well as their commitment to future growth and expansion. Once the senior leaders and I were satisfied with it, we scheduled a series of workshops for mid-level leaders to help them "connect the dots" between the broad company vision and their own day-to-day tasks and responsibilities. In other words, we showed how their work (and the work of their direct reports) supported the ongoing pursuit of the overall vision. *A beautifully written vision statement is useless unless people understand how it ties back to their work.*

3. **Low fidelity.** By "low fidelity," Nawaz is referring to scenarios in which "there's a written [vision] statement [but] decisions and individual actions are not aligned with the commitment communicated." This can occur when employees find themselves investing in unnecessary or trivial work that doesn't contribute toward the fulfillment of the vision.

Frequent check-ins with your people can be informative here. If an employee feels like all they're doing is trivial or meaningless work (remember the Progress Principle!), it's likely they will become disengaged. Of course, at one time or another, we all may need to engage in tedious but necessary work. What I'm referring to here is "busy work" — work that fills time and seems to serve no purpose. It's better to discover that an employee feels overloaded with busy work before their attitude and/or quality of work starts to suffer. Such conversations often surface areas of frustration you might otherwise be unaware of.

4. **Distaste.** Despite your best efforts to develop a vision that appeals to your entire team or organization, it's likely that someone, somewhere, will find it inadequate (recall the individual who challenged Steve Jobs). Rather than spend additional time honing the vision and fruitlessly seeking greater clarity, learn where the disconnect is for people. While you may discover that the vision could indeed be clearer, it's also possible that people are not buying into it for wholly different reasons.

I suggest going one step further and *soliciting the voices of your people in the development of the organizational or team vision.* After all, these are the individuals who need to be inspired by it. Not only will you gain buy-in by including them in the process, but they may offer ideas and suggestions that result in an even stronger vision.

5. **Work avoidance.** If your vision foments anxiety among your people because it promises more or different work for them, they may overtly (or subtly) choose to ignore it. Nawaz suggests leaders "look for ways to incentivize adoption of the [vision] and positively reward (even small) wins in the right direction." Such incentives may take the form of bonuses and other perks, or simply ongoing positive feedback and encouragement.

Several years ago, a large Philadelphia law firm hired me to lead an "innovation task force." The task force's purpose was to review the firm's operations and make recommendations to senior leadership regarding what could be improved to better serve clients. The first step I took was to help the team create a vision, that "North Star" that would define what success looked like for the team and help guide us there. We brainstormed for hours until we had flipcharts full of ideas displayed around the conference room. Next, we distilled the ideas into a few powerful, aspirational statements and illustrations that steered our thinking until the completion of the project. Interestingly, this firm was named one of the top U.S. law firms for innovation in 2018 (the year I worked with them). I'm not sure if the innovation task force's efforts directly or indirectly contributed to this honor, but I believe our results would have been less impactful without the time we invested in creating a clear and bold vision.

I once read that most change efforts fail because the people affected by the changes aren't committed to them. Again, if you craft a bold vision that makes people skeptical or anxious rather than energized, you've wasted your time. Affording people the opportunity to be involved in the creation of the vision (as I did with the law firm's innovation task force) is one way to get them invested. Nawaz's suggestion to grant bonuses and other perks to early adopters, or simply provide positive feedback and encouragement, are also worth considering. I'm also an advocate for publicly recognizing those whose work exemplifies the vision (make sure they're comfortable with public praise first) and for leveraging the Progress Principle by celebrating milestones and "small wins" toward adopting the vision.

Developing a Vision

Now that you know what a vision is and why it's critical to establish a compelling one for your team or organization, you may be wondering how to develop your own. While the process of developing a vision is unique to every team and organization, I'll share a few nuggets here for you to consider:

Think future. Don't confuse mission and vision. A *mission* defines what an organization does today, how it does it, and who it does it for. A *vision* is future-focused. As I mentioned earlier, it typically contains aspirational language and defines an as-yet-unrealized ideal state. Some of my favorite visions include:

- Cleveland Clinic: "To be the world's leader in patient experience, clinical outcomes, research and education."

- Hilton Worldwide: "To fill the earth with the light and warmth of hospitality."
- Best Friends Animal Society: "A better world through kindness to animals."
- Southwest Airlines: "To become the World's Most Loved, Most Flown, and Most Profitable Airline."

Think big. The hit song "Dreamer" by British band Supertramp asks: "Can you do something out of this world?" That question is at the heart of every great vision. The Cleveland Clinic's vision, for example, is to be the *world's* leader, not Cleveland's leader or even America's leader. There's nothing meek or mild about that vision. It's bold and confident, even audacious. Yours should be too.

Think visual. Developing a vision is the perfect opportunity to use arts-based learning (i.e., the use of artistic skills, methods, and experiences to enhance learning in areas *outside* of the arts). My doctoral dissertation was on arts-based learning and how the arts tap into our emotions in ways that defy rationality, often leading to startling "ah-ha" moments of discovery. For example, try starting your journey toward crafting a vision with pictures rather than words. The power of illustrations to elicit creative insights and generate new connections is remarkable (I personally witnessed this with the law firm's innovation task force). Get a piece of paper and a box of crayons or markers and unleash your imagination!

Think collaboration. Developing a vision is viewed by some as the job of senior leaders. It shouldn't be. When voices throughout the organization have an opportunity to contribute, the vision naturally becomes more inclusive and reflective of the entire culture. While senior leaders may ultimately *refine* the vision, the input of multiple perspectives throughout the creation process is key to creating a vision in which everyone feels invested.

Think communication. Rarely are visions — even great ones — adequately communicated throughout the organization. Consequently, they remain nebulous concepts that few employees devote much thought to. This is unfortunate. It is *every* leader's responsibility, from the CEO to frontline supervisors, to integrate the vision into the organization's DNA through every available communication channel. And while cafeteria posters are nice, they're no substitute for ongoing dialogue that makes explicit the connection between people's work and the company vision. It's at that nexus where people's hearts are won or lost.

Grand Finale

Look around your own team or organization. Is there a palpable sense of energy? Do people walk the corridors with a sense of purpose? Can you hear laughter emanating from meeting rooms? Are people's eyes bright or glazed over? Depending on your answer, it may be worth recalling the words of legendary jazz vocalist Ella Fitzgerald: "It isn't where you came from; it's where you're going that counts." That's the power of possibility. That's the power of vision. That's the power of direction.

Creating your team or organizational vision is an exercise where you'll want to "go big or go home." Take the time to do it with excellence. With the right team, goals, and messaging, your vision will permeate all aspects of your corporate culture and set the tone for the future of your workplace for years to come.

Now It's Your Turn: Which of the ideas presented in this chapter are resonating most? Why?

You've read the chapter—now get the tool! Download "Chart Your Course: Developing a Team Direction" and continue your personal development at

rightchordleadership.com/book-resources/

Note 6: Support

*Coaching, ongoing feedback, and encouragement motivate people
to continually improve and see obstacles as challenges to
overcome rather than permanent roadblocks.*

At long last we've reached the sixth and final note of the CHORDS Model—Support. When you routinely play this note along with the other five, your team or organization will perform as magnificently and dependably as a hand-crafted musical instrument.

Why is this note so important? I've seen research suggesting that feeling cared for by one's manager has a more significant impact on people's sense of trust and safety than any other leader behavior. Coaching, ongoing constructive feedback, and encouragement motivate people to pursue stretch goals, take sensible risks, learn from mistakes, and see problems as surmountable. In fact, without unwavering support from you, it's unlikely your employees will reach their full potential.

I'm continually surprised by the number of leaders who don't realize the importance of providing support to their team or organization. They invest a ton of energy ensuring processes and systems run efficiently while seeming to forget that *people are at the heart of their business.* In their book *The Progress Principle*, Drs. Teresa Amabile and Steven Kramer describe "support" as a *nourisher*, something that amplifies the meaning of work by making the recipient feel valued and important. As the saying goes, "You don't build a business. You build people and then *people* build the business." Support is a critical component of that progression.

Coaching

As a leader, you have many tools at your disposal to support your people effectively. Let's start with coaching, one of the most important in the emerging leader's toolkit. You don't need to be in the workforce for decades to be somebody's coach. I believe that if you possess the ability to assess some-body's performance with honesty and objectivity—and pro-vide constructive feedback intended to help that individual succeed—you can be a coach. Although professional leader-ship coaches do exist, I prefer to think of "coach" as a role that virtually anyone within an organization can adopt, rather than as a specific title or position.

Take a moment to think of a great coach in *your* life, some-one who was focused on strengthening or eliminating specific behaviors of yours. What were the circumstances? What char-acteristics or behaviors made them such an influential coach? In what way(s) did you benefit?

Did you just think of a sports coach? Our minds usually go to sports teams from our past when we think of coaches who impacted us. Sports coaches can indeed be some of the most impactful individuals in our lives. But great coaches aren't limited to the world of athletics. They can be parents, siblings, family members, neighbors, friends, teachers, col-leagues—anyone who has influenced you in a positive way and has your success at heart.

Being a good coach starts with a particular mindset, an attitude, that is defined by the strong desire to help others achieve. This mindset is not something you can turn off and on like a faucet. You either have it or you don't. It's OK if you don't, but don't expect to be a great coach—or even a good coach—without it.

My favorite definition of coaching comes from Sir John Whitmore's book *Coaching for Performance:*

> Coaching is unlocking a person's potential to maximize their own performance. *It is helping them to learn rather than teaching them.*

Perhaps this seems like a purely academic distinction. After all, isn't helping someone to learn the *same* as teaching them?

No, it's not. And herein lies the essence of coaching.

When you *teach* someone, you take knowledge from your own brain and "place" it into theirs. Your biology teacher, for example, "placed" knowledge about the workings of the human cell into your own brain—knowledge you didn't already possess. But when you *coach* someone, the assumption is that the knowledge *is already inside the other person and just needs to be coaxed out.*

I think of a coach as a *guide* (rather than a teacher) leading the employee to their own insights. You are, as Whitmore suggests, *helping them to learn rather than teaching them.* As such, coaching requires different skills than teaching. One could argue that the ideal leader is *both* teacher and coach and knows when to adopt either role depending on the situation.

As mentioned above, it makes sense that when we think about coaches, we may first recall coaches from the world of athletics. After all, coaches are an integral part of practically every sport, from individual sports like tennis and golf to team sports like basketball and baseball. In some respects, sports coaches and leader-coaches are similar. For example, both seek to elicit optimal performance by providing advice, making observations, and offering encouragement.

But sports coaches and leader-coaches differ in many important ways. Perhaps the most obvious difference is the way they *provide* coaching. Many sports coaches yell at players, shout at referees, pace the sidelines scowling, and use fear and intimidation as motivational tools. While this approach may be effective in a sports context, in my experience it is hardly ever effective in a business context. While athletes may tolerate a tough, even abusive coach if it results in more wins, most employees will not. In fact, adopting the mindset of a "win at all costs" sports coach in the workplace will likely have a detrimental effect on your team's overall performance, not to mention crush morale, trust, and engagement. I don't recommend it. The workplace is not a sports arena; a different coaching philosophy is needed.

Coaching should be thoughtful, purposeful, and meant to help the employee succeed. Unlike sports coaches, leader-coaches should never belittle, humiliate, or raise their voices. Here's an easy way to remember what coaching is all about:

> *If you're not coaching to improve performance in a respectful, patient, and helpful fashion, you're not coaching.*

One more important point: coaching is *not* counseling. *Coaching* is about performance improvement, professional development, and helping the employee reach their potential.

Counseling is about dealing with mental or emotional issues that—unless you have a degree in counseling or a related field—are best left to professionals.

Coaching	Counseling
Addresses specific work-related issues such as goal setting, skills development, and on-the-job performance	Focuses on emotional, psychological, and mental health issues
May involve exploring strengths and liabilities related to performance as well as alternative behaviors that can facilitate greater workplace effectiveness	May involve working through past traumas and negativity to help clients reach new insights and cope with lingering emotional damage
Typically focused on the present and future	Typically focused on the past and present
Can be done "in the moment" (no scheduling necessary)	Usually done over a period that may encompass months or even years
A coaching session can last a few minutes	A counseling session can last an hour or more

Figure 3

As a leader, you'll need to discern which employee issues are *coaching* issues and which are *counseling* issues. Your own manager or HR department can help you, if necessary.

Being a Great Leader-Coach

Now that you know what coaching is and isn't, we need to consider: What do great leader-coaches actually *do?* Let's answer that question with a baseball analogy.

Imagine a player, Scott, practicing his swing as the coach looks on. The coach notices a flaw in the player's grip on the bat and initiates a conversation.

"Why do you think you're not hitting the ball well, Scott?" the coach asks.

"I'm not sure," replies Scott.

"Do you think it's your stance, your eyesight, or your grip on the bat?"

Scott hesitates. "Umm, my grip?"

"Why do you think that?"

"Well, I think my stance and my eyes are fine."

"OK. If you think your problem is your grip, what might you do differently?"

"I could try holding the bat less tightly."

"OK, let's try that next game and see what happens."

Sounds ridiculous, right? No baseball coach would talk to a player this way. Rather, the coach would immediately point out the deficiency, recommend a different grip, and likely work with the player to master the new skill. That's the nature of coaching in the world of athletics: Identify the problem and provide a solution—fast!

Leader-coaching works differently. Sure, the goal is optimal performance just as in sports, but good leader-coaches don't *tell* employees what to do as much as they *draw the solution out of them*. In short, they guide the employee to their own insights by asking good questions and debating the merits of alternative behaviors. This approach is far more powerful, I believe, than simply telling the employee the right answer.

I encourage you to watch a video clip on YouTube of Benjamin Zander, the current musical director of the Boston Philharmonic Orchestra and the Boston Philharmonic Youth Orchestra, coaching a young cellist. Zander asks the student to play a piece by Bach, which the student does quite capably.

Zander praises his playing, then proceeds to ask him a series of questions designed to guide the student to *his own insights* about his performance. After a few minutes of coaching, Zander asks the student to play the same piece again. It is noticeably improved the second time.

It's important to note (no pun intended) that Zander never seizes the cello and says "Play it like *this*" before performing the piece himself. Merely by asking deft questions and offering continuous feedback, *he draws the correct technique out of the student rather than simply telling him what and how to play.* By guiding the student to his own insights and giving the student ownership of his learning process, Zander ensures the young musician's learning will "stick." In Whitmore's words, he helps the student to learn rather than teaching him: Zander presumed the capacity for a better performance *was already inside the young man.* It just needed to be extracted.

Now *that's* great coaching!

Of course, there are times when an employee needs to be told to do something in a particular way:

- "I need you to complete the weekly reports *like this* . . ."
- "I need you to create your PowerPoint slides *like this* . . ."
- "I need you to answer the phone *like this* . . ."
- "I need you to operate this piece of equipment *like this* . . ."

Where and when appropriate, telling an employee how to do something is perfectly OK (as long as it's done respectfully). *But it isn't coaching.* As a leader, you should learn to discern which situations call for "telling/teaching" and which for "coaching."

In addition to guiding employees to their own insights like Zander does, the most effective leader-coaches take at least *some* accountability for the poor performance of their direct reports.

What exactly does *that* look like?

For starters, when an employee is struggling, great leader-coaches don't sit back and allow them to fail. They recognize that a struggling employee is a reflection of their own leadership (or lack thereof) and summon the courage to ask some difficult but necessary questions. I recommend viewing a YouTube video by organizational psychologist, researcher, and *New York Times* best-selling author Dr. Tasha Eurich in which she identifies four questions leader-coaches should ask when dealing with a poor performer. Accountable leader-coaches ask *all four* questions, but they pay particular attention to the *last* one.

If you are currently dealing with a poor performer, take a few moments to record your response to each of Dr. Eurich's four questions. Doing so may help you discover contributing factors you were previously unaware of:

- Does the employee understand my expectations?
- Is there something outside their control affecting performance?
- Does the employee know that they are not meeting expectations?
- Am I contributing to this problem?

Question 1 concerns the clarity of your **communication**. It's the first Note of the CHORDS Model.

Question 2 touches on Notes 3 (**Ownership**) and 4 (**Respect**). By asking this question, you are acknowledging that the employee may be attempting to be **accountable** but is potentially contending with external factors that are compromising their performance. You are also demonstrating **respect** by being open to this possibility and not jumping to conclusions.

Question 3 encompasses Note 1 again (**Communication**) as well as Note 6 (**Support**). If the employee is unaware that they're not meeting expectations, you may need to have an honest conversation and/or engage in some **coaching.**

Question 4 is all about **self-awareness** (emotional intelligence). Self-aware leaders are not afraid to consider the possibility that *they* may be contributing to an employee's poor performance in some way.

Feedback

Another quality that distinguishes great leader-coaches is their skill at delivering high-quality *feedback*. Feedback can take many forms, but it's essentially the sharing of information that is intended to help the employee's performance improve. When providing feedback, what you say is important. But *how* you say it is just as important.

As we discussed earlier, displays of temper and aggression may work in athletics but are almost certain to be ineffective in organizations. In all my years as a consultant, I've never met anyone who responded positively to being chewed out. Great leader-coaches understand that effective feedback is thoughtful, honest, and intended to help the employee improve. Feedback intended to intimidate, embarrass, or instill fear is still technically feedback, but it's not part of coaching as I envision it.

Here is my Golden Rule of Feedback: Before you provide it, check your intentions. If you are providing feedback for any reason *other than* helping your employee succeed, stop and think. You may be doing more harm than good.

Some leaders believe providing feedback once a year at annual review time is sufficient. It isn't. Imagine a professional athlete receiving feedback from their coaches only once a year, or a student receiving feedback from their teachers only once a year. Why would it be different for employees? Feedback—constructive, helpful, thoughtful feedback—should be given frequently but *not so frequently* that it becomes annoying. There is no formula that dictates how often to provide it, so use your discretion. If you feel you may be overdoing it, you probably are.

Keep in mind that constructive feedback is *not* the same as criticism. Constructive feedback is intended to *improve* performance while criticism — the expression of disapproval based on perceived faults or mistakes — usually just makes the other person feel bad. For leader-coaches, this distinction is important.

Interlude: Remembering Stevie Ray Vaughan

Guitar virtuoso Stevie Ray Vaughan died tragically in a helicopter crash in 1990. Although I'm not a guitarist, I have always appreciated and admired Vaughan's incredible skill, passion, and artistry. Vaughan's playing has influenced countless guitarists, of course, but it was an incident from 1982 that really piqued my attention. It happened when Vaughan and his band, Double Trouble, performed at the 1982 Montreux Jazz Festival and were booed by a handful of ornery audience members.

Dan Opperman, the band's road manager, recalls: "Stevie was pretty disappointed. [He] just handed me his guitar and walked off stage, and I'm like, 'Are you coming back?' He went back to the dressing room with his head in his hands."

Vaughan himself later said of the incident: "It wasn't the whole crowd [that booed]. It was just a few people sitting right up front. The room there was built for acoustic jazz. When five or six people boo, wow. It sounds like the whole world hates you. They thought we were too loud, but shoot, I had four army blankets folded over my amp, and the volume level was on 2. I'm used to playin' on 10!"

If evidence was ever needed that you can't please everybody no matter how hard you try, I'm sure nothing could top the booing of Stevie Ray Vaughan. But it's worth noting that Vaughan didn't allow himself to stay down. The next night, Jackson Browne was in the audience and offered Vaughan the use of his studio for free (resulting in Double Trouble's 1983 debut album, *Texas Flood*). David Bowie also got wind of Vaughan's talent and hired him to play on his 1983 album, *Let's Dance*, as well as the subsequent tour.

Criticism is tough—for gifted guitarists and leaders alike. But the great ones receive critical feedback openly and thoughtfully (even when it's not tactfully delivered), incorporate the nuggets of truth, and move on. It's not easy, but personal growth rarely is. As Winston Churchill said, "Criticism may not be agreeable, but it is necessary. It fulfills the same function as pain in the human body; it calls attention to the development of an unhealthy state of things."

I've always been grateful to Vaughan for his exceptional music. Decades after his death, I'm grateful for the reminder that nobody can bring you down unless you let them.

What Great Musicians Know About Giving Constructive Feedback

If public speaking is our #1 fear and death is #2 (as comedian Jerry Seinfeld once pointed out in one of his stand-up specials), giving constructive feedback may just be #3. It stands to reason why so many of us are reluctant to offer constructive feedback: most people aren't receptive to it. Reactions can range from minor disagreement to tears, personal attacks, or worse. How can we increase our chances of a productive feedback session?

In an HBR article, author Holly Weeks states, "When delivering negative feedback to someone who's likely to get defensive, it's not your job to make the other person feel better. It's your job to deliver the information in a clear, neutral, and temperate way." As I read the article, it occurred to me that great musicians—many of whom are also great coaches—do this very well.

Take renowned violinist Itzhak Perlman, for example. In my coaching workshop, I show a YouTube video of Perlman interacting with young Russian musicians during a master class. His feedback technique is superb: Rather than focus on what the students do wrong, he focuses on how they can play *better*. To one student, Perlman says: "Don't play fast between the sections. Take your time. Wait until the sound comes out. . . . When you wait, you'll really say to the people, 'Isn't this beautiful?'" The student smiles broadly, imagining the scene Perlman has painted.

With another student, Perlman laces his comments with humor. Pointing to the curled end of his own violin and moving it in an exaggeratedly wide circle, he says, "It's like you have a pencil here and you're trying to draw a picture." Both student and audience crack up. Perlman is a master of putting students at ease with his warm demeanor and gentle manner.

Giving constructive feedback need not be a source of anxiety for the giver or the receiver. While we can't control the other person's reaction, we can surely calibrate our feedback in a way that mitigates defensiveness. The next time you need to provide constructive feedback, consider taking a page out of Perlman's playbook. Keep it clear, neutral, and temperate, and chances are you'll hit all the right notes.

Three Steps to Effective Feedback

The first step in providing effective feedback is **Preparation**. Here are eight tips to consider:

1. **Think it through.** As a leader, you may occasionally need to give feedback in the moment (i.e., immediately after observing a particular behavior). In other cases,

you may need to schedule a more formal meeting. No matter whether your feedback is brief or more extensive, never deliver it without first thinking through what you want to say. Providing constructive feedback to an employee can be a delicate matter and needs to be taken seriously. Spend some time beforehand planning your approach—even if it's just a few minutes. Anticipate resistance and reflect on your responses. You'll find this to be time well spent.

2. **Identify *precisely* what the issue is and consider what might be causing it.** Ambiguity has no place in a feedback session. For example, "Your work needs to improve" or "You need to do better" are far too vague to be effective. Be clear and concise in your assessment: "I've noticed an increase in errors in your weekly reports and want to discuss why it's happening and how we can correct it."

   Once you've identified the key issue or concern, consider what might be *causing* it. Has anything changed recently in terms of processes or protocols? Have you noticed any other behavioral changes with the employee? Remember Dr. Eurich's four questions from earlier. This is a good time in the process to think through them.

3. **As you consider causes and possible solutions, avoid getting locked into "tunnel vision."** This can happen when you convince yourself that you know *for certain* why something is happening without considering *other* possibilities. There may be factors at play you don't know about. Be open and receptive to alternative

explanations that can arise during the coaching conversation.

4. **Watch your assumptions.** It's easy to make assumptions about others when their performance is lacking: "She's lazy" or "He's not a team player." Don't do it. Assumptions may *feel* right but are often proven inaccurate once more information is gathered. Indisputable data ("I've noted that you were late three times this week by at least a half hour") will strengthen your position more than assumptions about the other person's intentions or character.

5. **As best you can, compute the cost of the employee's behavior in both financial and human terms.** If it's the case that the behavior is affecting productivity, be prepared to show *how* it's being affected. For example, indicate how the employee's errors are costing precious time because of the rework required to fix them.

   If the behavior is affecting something less concrete (such as team morale), quantifying the cost of the behavior may be more challenging. It's still possible, though. You might say, "My sense is that these frequent errors are negatively impacting the entire team." Then provide evidence to support your contention.

6. **Expect to be challenged.** The first thing the employee is likely to do is challenge your assertion(s). The challenge may be emphatic, or it may simply be a request for examples. If you have no evidence, your credibility will take a hit. You don't need pages and pages of data, but you should be prepared to back up your position.

7. **Keep it positive.** It may be counterintuitive to suggest that a conversation about a performance issue should be positive—but it's true! As I've stressed, this is *not* an opportunity to criticize the employee with vague accusations; rather, it's a chance to discuss how a *particular aspect* of their overall performance can be improved. It's also an opportunity to discuss specific areas where the employee is doing well, so come prepared with those too.

8. **Consider where the coaching takes place.** The setting of the conversation can have a significant impact on the outcome. For example, an office or conference room may afford maximum privacy but can also be intimidating. Use your discretion. Sometimes the informal nature of a "coffee chat" can decrease anxiety and facilitate a fruitful discussion.

    While I prefer in-person coaching meetings whenever possible, virtual coaching is certainly an option. Just be sure to remove any distractions in your immediate environment and be especially attuned to the employee's nonverbal cues (tone of voice, facial expressions, etc.).

The second step in the feedback delivery process is to effectively **Calibrate the Conversation**. Keep these three tips in mind:

1. **Listen carefully.** A wise person once said we have one mouth and two ears because we should do *twice* as much listening as talking. That's good advice. Always

allow the employee an opportunity to respond to your feedback. Your conception of what happened may be considerably different from theirs. When the employee offers their perspective, don't interrupt. This exchange should be a dialogue, not a monologue.

2. **Respond thoughtfully.** Remember: coaching is about helping the employee succeed. A harsh or degrading response will cause the employee to become defensive, shut down, or both. Ask questions without using an accusatory tone and show that you're open to other interpretations or explanations as long as they're reasonable. You should adopt the mindset of a detective gathering information rather than that of an army general demanding obedience.

3. **Resist imposing your own solution.** As I stated earlier, coaching is not about *telling* someone what to do. It's about guiding the employee to their own insights with your support and encouragement. That's not to say you shouldn't ever offer advice or make recommendations based on your own experience. But it's important to explore possible solutions *together* until you land on one that feels good to both of you.

Once you reach agreement on what is causing the performance issue and possible solutions, it's time for the third step: **Identifying Next Steps**. Consider the following tips:

1. **Record some goals on paper.** They should include clear targets and the behaviors necessary to reach them. "Improve attitude" or "Reduce errors," for

example, are poorly articulated goals because they are too vague. What will an improved attitude look like in terms of *behaviors?* What is an acceptable number of errors going forward? Ten? Five? Zero? Be specific. There should be no ambiguity here: You and your employee need to reach an understanding of *exactly* what is expected and what next steps need to be taken.

2. **Ask "What more can I do to help you?"** I believe this is one of the most powerful questions a leader can ask. Doing so demonstrates your belief that helping your employees succeed is an integral part of your job. If the employee asks for something you cannot provide, explain why. Be sure to carry through on any agreements and/or promises you make. Failing to follow up on an employee's request can erode trust and damage your relationship.

3. **Recap the meeting to ensure you and the employee are on the same page.** A quick summary (even just a couple of minutes) can prevent future misunderstandings and should take place *before* you conclude the meeting. Say something like, "Before we finish up, let's summarize what we've covered today and what comes next."

4. **Keep the dialogue going.** Check in periodically with the employee to see how he or she is faring or agree to meet on a more formal basis until the issue is resolved. Always acknowledge progress (remember the Progress Principle) and express appreciation for ongoing improvement. Research suggests that providing appreciation and affirming feedback positively impacts employee performance.

Recognition

A great way to play the Support note through feedback is to offer recognition and appreciation. In my experience, managers tend to *overestimate* how much they offer recognition and *underestimate* how important it is to employees. Furthermore, research shows that failing to provide adequate recognition *suppresses* the behavior you want from your employee. Imagine that you coach someone to change a particular behavior, and they do so successfully. However, you don't offer at least some recognition or acknowledgment in return. Their willingness to maintain the new behavior may be dampened considerably; they may even revert to the old behavior!

Everyone craves recognition for doing a good job; even a simple "thank you" can suffice (although I suggest being more specific). When you offer recognition, praise, or appreciation on a frequent basis, you'll discover that others are more willing to do what you ask of them.

Here are a few ways to recognize your people and keep the note of Support pitch-perfect on your team:

- Emails are fine, but handwritten notes are better. Employees tend to keep them, often for years.
- Take time during team meetings to publicly acknowledge individuals for their recent good work (be sure to ask for permission first as some folks are uncomfortable with public praise).
- Provide enough recognition so that any *constructive* feedback you give won't be dismissed as "the usual criticism."

- Start the day with five coins in your pocket and transfer a coin to the other side when you offer recognition. Try to get all five coins to the other pocket!

None of the excuses some leaders use for *not* providing recognition hold water with me. Let's look at a few:

- **Excuse: "Employees shouldn't be thanked for doing what we pay them to do."**
  Paying people doesn't absolve managers of the responsibility to offer recognition when it's deserved. This doesn't mean thanking employees for accomplishing routine tasks (although there's nothing wrong with it), but it *does* mean acknowledging them when they do something noteworthy.

- **Excuse: "It's not in my personality."**
  Offering recognition doesn't require a particular personality. It simply requires an awareness of its importance to people and the positive impact it has on job performance.

- **Excuse: "I have too many direct reports."**
  You don't have to offer *every* employee recognition *every* day. But no matter how many direct reports you have, you should find time in your week to reach as many as you can. Claiming you have too many direct reports to offer recognition is a poor excuse.

- **Excuse: "I don't get recognized by *my* boss."**
  This is no reason to avoid recognizing your own people. Why emulate poor behavior? Good leaders do the right thing regardless of what others do.

- **Excuse: "They don't do anything praiseworthy."**
  A lack of praiseworthy accomplishments or behavior is a reflection on *you*. The first thing a leader who uses this excuse should do is ask, "What's my role here?" *They* are likely the problem.

Interlude: Lessons from Whiplash

> *"You get the best effort from others not by lighting a fire beneath them, but by building a fire within." — Bob Nelson, author*

If you saw the 2014 movie *Whiplash*, you'll surely remember Terence Fletcher (played by J. K. Simmons), the tyrannical jazz band leader fond of profanity and humiliating his young musicians. The film would have you believe this approach to teaching yields great performance, but that wasn't my experience when I was a member of my high school jazz band. In fact, the best band directors and music teachers I had took the *opposite* tack. They provided support not by screaming at and berating us but by inspiring us. They set a clear example of how to achieve success, provided clear and honest feedback, and continually challenged us to reach new heights week by week, month by month.

You and your organization have no doubt invested a lot of time and money finding the right employees. To enable them to achieve peak performance, don't follow the Fletcher model. Provide support the same way my music teachers did. Whether you realize it or not, your employees are looking to you to set the right example:

- **Be purposeful and methodical in your communication.** Employees frequently complain of having to sift through mountains of messages when only a few are truly important. In addition, vague or contradictory messages cause confusion and consume valuable time to interpret. As I stressed earlier, be crystal-clear in both your written and spoken communication.

- **Be willing to share your experiences, wisdom, and suggestions so that your employees can excel.** We don't always find the best way to do something the first time, and that's OK. Making mistakes is part of the journey and essential to learning. As leaders, we need to model the behaviors of success and how to rebound after setbacks.

- **Make accountability a key value of your team.** When I didn't practice properly for an upcoming lesson, my teachers didn't lose their temper. They expressed disappointment and told me I was capable of better. That was a far more powerful way to support me than criticizing me or yelling Fletcher style.

- **Ensure that you and your employees share the same goals.** Musicians need to be totally aligned in terms of their performance. If band members tried to play different pieces at the same time, for example, the result would be chaos. When leaders set and communicate specific goals, all employees work from the same "sheet music," so to speak.

- **Empower employees to take initiative and solve problems on their own.** Most employees (especially Millennials and Gen Z) want the freedom to be creative, take calculated risks, and try new things. You need to be prepared to encourage them. This doesn't mean allowing conduct that is inconsistent with organizational values and goals but rather nurturing autonomy, demonstrating confidence in their abilities, and providing coaching when necessary.

- **Providing recognition when your employees find a solution to a problem is great, but don't stop there.** Also acknowledge employees who identify a potential problem, as well as those who are making progress on finding a solution but haven't discovered it yet. Your employees will want to continue down the path of success when they know you appreciate their effort.

Achieving success as a musician is rooted in finding players who want to make the group as a whole sound good, not just themselves. It's the same with work teams. As a leader, you need to make sure your people are motivated and well prepared to meet the demands they face. It's not an easy job, and leadership isn't for everybody. But for those who accept the role, incorporating the previous suggestions as part of your repertoire is the best way I know to get your team performing at its peak.

A Word About Leading Millennials and Gen Z

Generational differences in the workplace can lead to significant misunderstandings if they're not effectively addressed.

Millennials (born between 1981 and 1996) make up a major portion of the workforce, and Gen Z (born between 1997 and

2012) will be entering the workforce in droves in the next few years. These demographic segments have been tagged with all kinds of labels, not all of them complimentary. Your success in leading and supporting them will depend on playing the right chords.

I know many young people who resent the popular stereotypes associated with them, and I want to be careful painting with too broad a brush. Not every millennial or Gen Zer, of course, falls neatly into the descriptions below. However, adhering to the following suggestions consistently can help you leverage the unique skills of your younger workers and establish team harmony:

1. **More feedback more often.** Young people—many of whom are ambitious, career-focused, and willing to improve to get ahead—may be accustomed to feedback from parents, teachers, guidance counselors, and coaches. Consequently, they'll expect it at their job. If they don't receive it, they may start searching for an employer where feedback is shared more frequently (as long as it is delivered with respect and tact).

2. **Make feedback constructive.** Don't just point out performance gaps and move on; provide substantive feedback that helps the employee course-correct with confidence. When I worked at QVC years ago, a coach praised how I'd facilitated the first part of a training program. Referring to a different piece of content, he made a suggestion about how I could do even better. "That piece was good," he said of the first part. "I liked

what you did. But you might want to try this . . ." Talk about playing the right chords! He didn't make me feel like a failure; rather, he gave me solid advice intended to improve my performance. I still remember it more than two decades later.

3. **Provide feedback quickly.** Feedback offered days or weeks after an incident loses its power and fosters resentment: "Now you're telling me?!" I suggest waiting no more than 24 hours to provide feedback.

4. **Make feedback coach-centric.** Bullying, intimidation, and humiliation are relics of the past. These techniques may have worked with earlier generations, but millennials and Gen Zers will head for the exits if they feel attacked. Mistakes are a natural part of learning—yes, feedback should be honest, but it should also be thoughtful, diplomatic, and focused on success.

5. **Ask for their input.** When it comes to feedback, your employees' perspectives are just as important as yours. So don't crush millennials and Gen Zers with a "firehose" of feedback. Use four of the most powerful words in a leader's vocabulary: "What do *you* think?" And remember that feedback should be a dialogue, not a diatribe.

6. **Reinforce the value of their work.** In their book *The Progress Principle*, Drs. Teresa Amabile and Steven Kramer noted that having a sense of meaning in one's work is a critical driver of engagement. For millennials and Gen Z in particular, this is especially true. Young employees want to feel that their work is making a

contribution to something more than earning a profit or raising the value of a stock.

7. **Help them see the "big picture."** Many young workers believe their employer is ineffective at helping them understand how their job fits into the company's overall goals. Because millennials and Gen Zers have relatively little work experience compared to older workers, they can have an especially limited view of what's happening beyond their own departments. Understanding the connection between one's work and the organization's overall mission and vision is a key driver of engagement.

8. **Connect with what they care about.** If a young employee displays affinity for a particular aspect of your team's work, such as interacting with customers, discuss it with them. Perhaps doing more of that will lead to a renewed sense of energy and enthusiasm for the job.

9. **Acknowledge contributions.** Younger workers can quickly become disengaged if they receive a steady stream of corrective feedback and no praise. You don't need to shower them with accolades, but regularly showing appreciation for their efforts will nourish their self-confidence.

10. **Celebrate "small wins."** Drs. Amabile and Kramer assert that celebrating small wins—small, incremental steps toward achieving a larger goal—can yield significant psychological benefits for employees. Younger workers may not experience many triumphant

breakthrough moments at their jobs, but they almost certainly experience various forms of progress. Look for opportunities to acknowledge not only the achievement of a goal but the milestones along the way.

11. **Encourage innovative thinking.** In her article titled "Fortunately The Largest Workforce In History Is The Most Creative: The Millennials," Claudia Gioia writes: "It's not a surprise that most of the successful and innovative businesses are powered by Millennials: Google, Facebook, Snapchat, Airbnb, to name a few. The culture of these companies is to have a workforce of young people who welcome the creation of new ideas on a constant basis." My experience with millennials and Gen Zers mirrors Gioia's — they readily challenge the status quo and seek new processes, procedures, and systems that will improve organizational performance. An organization that puts the brakes on innovation may find its younger workers fleeing for more progressive companies.

12. **Encourage exploratory conversations.** The worst thing you can do when a millennial or Gen Zer comes to you with a suggestion or new idea is dismiss it outright. "That kind of thing won't work here" and similar sentiments can easily douse the flames of inspiration. Your best move is to seek more information by asking good questions: How do you think this will help? What potential downsides exist? What resources will you need to move that idea forward? Listen with an "every idea is a good idea" mindset (there will be time to critique later).

13. **Watch out for strict rules that stifle creativity.** Of course, organizations have rules and protocols that must be followed. But within those parameters should be ample opportunity to explore and experiment. You don't need to install pool tables and beanbag chairs to spur creativity; simply send the message that fresh ideas are not only desired but encouraged and watch what happens. If an idea can't be implemented, explain why. Don't let it fall into a black hole of radio silence.

14. **Be clear with ends, flexible with means.** If you're going to allow for exploration and experimentation, do it right. I think this is especially true for young employees: provide clear goals, encouragement, and a dash of well-intentioned oversight, then stand back and watch 'em go.

15. **Encourage young employees to "own" their ideas.** When I was in my 20s, my best managers not only listened to my ideas but let me work on improving them after considering their feedback. When you afford young workers this type of autonomy, you build their business skills as well as their confidence. And if they make a mistake or two along the way, give them the tools and guidance to fix it themselves.

Top musicians reach peak performance with training and practice. It's the same for millennials and Gen Zers in the workplace. Younger workers are the most tech-savvy and socially active in history. Most are ambitious, receptive to coaching, and take genuine pride in their work. Don't let a talented employee walk out the door because you failed to play the right chords.

Five Tips for Supporting Your Boss

If the work of hundreds of songwriters throughout the decades is any indication, maintaining a good relationship with your boss can be challenging. How many of these classic, boss-hatin' lyrics do you know?

"You got me working, boss man / A-workin' around the clock / I want a little drink of whiskey / You sure won't let me stop." (The Grateful Dead's cover of "Big Boss Man")

"I ain't gonna work for no soul sucking jerk / I'm gonna take it all back / And I ain't saying jack / I ain't gonna work for no soul sucking jerk." (Beck's "Soul Suckin' Jerk")

"Well, I'm a-gonna raise a fuss, I'm a-gonna raise a holler / I've been working all summer just to try and earn a dollar / Well I went to the boss, said 'I got a date' / The boss said, 'No dice, son, you gotta work late.'" (The Who's cover of "Summertime Blues")

"9 to 5, for service and devotion / You would think that I would deserve a fair promotion / Want to move ahead but the boss won't seem to let me / I swear sometimes that man is out to get me." (Dolly Parton's "9 to 5")

These examples might leave listeners with negative feelings about bosses, and it's true that some are awful. But not all work relationships with managers or supervisors have to be this way. Having a strong, collaborative, supportive relationship with your boss might not be as hard as you think, and it can greatly improve your career.

Here are some noteworthy tips for building a good relationship with your boss:

- Some people are naturally sunny and cheerful, others are typically dour, and still others may bounce from mood to mood unpredictably. There's not much you can do to change someone's temperament (i.e., the way they usually are), but you can learn to read your boss's day-to-day social cues. "The best thing you can do for your boss's mood is act as you normally do," writes Lauren Berger on fastcompany.com. "Be the consistent force they can rely on. Don't let your boss's mood affect you." Easier said than done, perhaps, but it's important not to let your boss's foul mood get under your skin.

- Effective communication is critical to a positive relationship with your boss, so get familiar with her communication style. How does she like to get information—email, printed reports, or in person? Does she tend to be verbose or reserved? Does she speak at a fast or slow pace? You don't need to become a communications expert to assess how your boss wants information conveyed, but if you're not sure, ask.

- No matter how you feel toward your boss, showing respect is crucial. You may feel he is not deserving of respect—and you may be right—but that kind of attitude will only make things worse. We can't control the chords others play at work, but we can always control our own. Consequently, I always seek to engage others according to *my* values and personal standards, not someone else's. When I respond to rudeness with courtesy, or disrespect with respect, I am the bigger person. As actress Mia Farrow once said, "I'm going to take the high road because the low road is too crowded."

- Have the courage to express yourself openly and honestly to your boss. But don't just barge into her office and start complaining. Plan your approach. Think about how you will start the conversation. Anticipate where there might be resistance and prepare effective responses. Practice keeping your composure. Fear prevents many of us from having difficult but necessary conversations with bosses, but when we do, things typically go OK. However, if things do go awry, stand up for yourself. "If you fold up under the pressure of a mean boss, the boss is then given the sword to take you out of the game," says Don Hurzeler, author of *The Way Up: How to Keep Your Career Moving in the Right Direction*. "The mean boss wins and you lose."

- Lastly, make a habit of regularly asking how you can better support your boss. Consider that she is likely getting squeezed by multiple stakeholders; demonstrating that her success is a priority of yours will strengthen the relationship and create that feeling of trust and camaraderie we all seek.

You don't have to be best friends with your boss, but being communicative, accountable, and proactive will go a long way toward creating a mutually rewarding relationship. Always be mindful of the chords you play, stay true to your values, ask for feedback, and have the courage of your convictions. Ultimately, if your current boss isn't willing to do their part in forging that high-quality relationship, find one who is.

Grand Finale

Early in Flip Like Wilson's career, we worked with a performance coach named Michael Stratford who'd garnered a considerable following among local bands in the Philadelphia region. His workshops were exceedingly popular, and his ability to help bands reach their artistic potential was highly respected.

Our work with Michael was transformative. He showed us how to confront and overcome our fears and doubts, lay bare the emotional core of a song, and communicate those emotions to the audience with laser-like intensity. Using unconventional team building and listening exercises, he illustrated the importance of each band member's contribution to the success of the unit. Perhaps most importantly, he underscored the need to always support and encourage one another, no matter what the circumstances.

I remember an exercise where Michael had each band member recite the lyrics of a song of our choosing out loud. The other members were instructed to raise their hands once they felt the words had connected with them on a deep emotional level. Until then, they were to sit quietly and listen. I recall reciting my song over and over, hoping to see raised hands but instead receiving no reaction. Finally, after an embarrassing number of attempts, the hands went up. I was exhausted and, to be honest, a bit frustrated.

"That right there is what I need from you every night," said Michael, smiling. Almost 30 years later, I can still remember his voice. Michael's guidance has been invaluable to me, both on stage as a musician and in my career as a consultant, trainer, speaker, and educator. He helped me understand myself better and opened my eyes to new possibilities. I try to do the same for my clients with the same generosity, grace, and authenticity as Michael. I hope I do it half as well as he did.

As this chapter concludes, I suggest taking a few moments now to answer this question: As a leader, what can you start, stop, or continue doing to become a better coach? Improving your coaching and feedback skills can provide the support necessary to help your people reach the next level of excellence. Start today with the tips and techniques covered here. Remember: we are not born great coaches. Good coaching takes diligence, discipline, and practice!

Now It's Your Turn: Which of the ideas presented in this chapter are resonating most? Why?

You've read the chapter—now get the tool! Unlock additional insights by downloading "Empowering Your Team: The Leader's Role in Providing Support" at

rightchordleadership.com/book-resources/

Completing The Octave:
Creativity and Innovation

While creativity and innovation are not part of the CHORDS Model, I would be remiss if I didn't include a discussion of them in this book. Think of them as the final two notes in an octave (i.e., a common musical interval consisting of eight notes) that begins with the six notes of the CHORDS Model. While those six notes are unequivocally crucial to success, truly elite organizations and teams also make time and space for creativity (Note 7) and innovation (Note 8) to flourish.

Creativity and innovation are often used interchangeably, but they are not the same. Simply put, *creativity* is the generation of new ideas while *innovation* is the practical application of those ideas (i.e., bringing those ideas to life). If I conjure up an idea for solving a particular problem, I am being creative. If I can then bring that idea to fruition in the form of a new product, process, or service, then I am being innovative.

Some of the most creative and innovative people who ever lived are musicians (OK, maybe I'm a little biased). What follows are a collection of "greatest hits" — examples of creativity and innovation from the world of music that shed light on the creative mindset and the innovative spirit. I encourage you to reflect on them and "connect the dots" to your own work. I'm confident you'll find these nuggets of wisdom not only enjoyable but enlightening and inspiring.

Decades Later, Lessons from *Ten* Still Resonate

Pearl Jam's classic debut album *Ten* was not an immediate success upon its release in 1991. However, by late 1992, it had reached number two on the Billboard 200 chart and helped usher in the alternative rock movement that would dominate popular music for the next few years. It is now widely considered one of the best rock albums of the '90s.

The story of how *Ten* came to be provides some insight into the creative process. One of my favorite stories concerns how singer Eddie Vedder came up with the lyrics. The unknown (at the time) singer hadn't slept for days when he decided to go surfing after listening to the demos provided by the fledgling band.

"I went surfing in [a] sleep-deprived state and totally started dealing with a few things that I hadn't dealt with," Vedder later said. "I was really getting focused on this one thing, and I had this music in my mind at the same time. I was literally writing some of these words as I was going up against a wave." Vedder dashed back to his apartment and recorded himself singing over three of the songs (two of which became monster hits "Alive" and "Once").

I'm not suggesting skipping a few nights' sleep to ignite your creativity (although that might work—I've never tried it). But getting out of familiar surroundings to engage in creative work can be highly productive. You don't have to go surfing, of course, but relocating to a similarly tranquil environment—away from endless interruptions, meetings, phone calls, and text messages—can foster unconventional mental connections and spark a wealth of insights. That's why a one-day team offsite can potentially yield the same quantity and quality of ideas as a week's worth of effort in the same old conference room. Even the simple act of walking can generate new ideas.

Getting out of your workspace occasionally to think creatively may not help you pen the next massive hit album. But chances are you will make some discoveries or identify opportunities you almost certainly wouldn't have otherwise.

What *Revolver* Teaches Us About Innovation

Many people believe *Revolver* is the Beatles' best album. A complete examination of this iconic work would fill thousands of pages; for now, I want to briefly focus on how the Beatles' approach to recording *Revolver* aligns with my thinking around creativity and innovation.

According to the album's recording engineer, Geoff Emerick, no preproduction or rehearsal process took place for *Revolver*; instead, the band created each song in the studio from what was often just a rough outline. The band also experimented with new sounds. According to the website the-paulmccartney-project.com, Emerick put it this way: "It was implanted when we started *Revolver* that every instrument should sound unlike itself: a piano shouldn't sound like a piano, a guitar shouldn't sound like a guitar." This led to the inclusion of uncommon instruments, such as the Indian tambura and tabla, clavichord, and vibraphone. Adding to the fresh approach was the use of new amplifiers, guitars, and limiters (a type of audio technology).

But the Beatles didn't stop there. For the first time in the band's output, *Revolver* saw the inclusion of a horn section (on "Got to Get You into My Life") and sound effects (on "Yellow Submarine"). Furthermore, the band incorporated a brand-new technology known as automatic double tracking (ADT): "This technique employed two linked tape recorders to automatically create a doubled vocal track" (Source: the-paulmccartney-project.com), replacing the need to sing the same piece twice to double a vocal part.

Want more *Revolver* innovations? Here are just a few:

- "Tomorrow Never Knows" marked the first time that a vocal was recorded with a microphone plugged into a Leslie speaker.
- The inclusion of reversed tape sounds on "Rain" marked the first pop release to use this technique.
- The backward (or "backmasked") guitar solo on "I'm Only Sleeping" was unprecedented in pop music at the time.
- The innovative way Emerick captured Ringo Starr's drums (by inserting an item of clothing inside the bass drum, among other things) forever changed the way drums were recorded.

"I know for a fact," said Emerick, "that from the day it came out, *Revolver* changed the way that everyone else made records." According to the website faroutmagazine.co.uk, Paul McCartney himself said, "There are sounds [on *Revolver*] that nobody else has done yet. I mean nobody . . . ever."

It's fun to revisit classic albums such as *Revolver* and admire the sheer audacity of their creators. But there's a larger lesson here: in business, as in music, experimentation, exploration, and risk-taking must play a role. While organizational protocols and procedures that limit behavior (what I call *constraining factors*) are necessary for any smooth-running operation, we tend to over-emphasize them while diminishing the importance of *liberating factors* that unleash creative energy. When was the last time you held a genuine brainstorming session to tackle a tough challenge? Took a calculated risk? Tried a new approach or process? Invited an outsider to a meeting? Granted your team time to talk about something other than work?

When Lennon and McCartney wrote "I was alone, I took a ride, I didn't know what I would find there / Another road where maybe I could see another kind of mind there" (from "Got to Get You into My Life"), they weren't referring to the innovation process. But they might as well have been. I challenge you to take that ride more often. Even if you don't create a *Revolver*-type revolution, you just might discover something amazing!

Beware the Folly of "Premature Dismissal"

No, I'm not talking about getting out of school early. I'm talking about dismissing a potentially viable idea because it doesn't conform to our current way of thinking. Examples of a premature dismissal (PD) include statements like these:

- "It'll never work."
- "That's not how we do things around here."
- "We tried that once before."
- "They'll never go for it."
- "I don't see it working for us."

One of my favorite examples of PD is described in the 2015 book *Van Halen Rising* by Greg Renoff (which I highly recommend if you like the band). It occurred back in 1976 when KISS manager Bill Aucoin had an opportunity to sign a very young Van Halen. Upon listening to their demo, however, Aucoin told the California foursome they had "no commercial potential" and passed. Some have called this decision the biggest blunder in A&R history given that Van Halen went on to become one of the highest-selling rock acts of all time.

I'm sure Aucoin had his reasons, but to quote French writer André Gide, "One does not discover new lands without consenting to lose sight of the shore." Sure, certain aspects of your business require consistency and uniformity in execution. But I suggest trying to make time every week to "lose sight of the shore," if only for a little while. When you unleash the power of "What if . . ." and "How might . . ." thinking, it's amazing what you can discover.

Why Outsider Perspectives Are Critical

Until seventh grade, the only genre of music I'd been exposed to was classical. When I discovered jazz that year, I transitioned from clarinet to sax in order to play in the school jazz band (jazz band was a clarinet-free zone). Because it's such a versatile instrument, learning the sax greatly broadened my musical palette. I still listened to Beethoven and Mozart, but now I sought out musicians from the worlds of jazz, R&B, pop, funk, and rock to develop my sound and technique.

Opening my ears to previously unfamiliar musical styles made me a more well-rounded saxophonist and helped me become a more in-demand player. One of my musical heroes, the great John Coltrane, also borrowed from other musical genres, in particular Indian music and the work of sitarist and composer Ravi Shankar.

The value of remaining open to ideas from outside your industry cannot be overstated. I argue that leaders should go as far afield as possible without completely losing touch or becoming disconnected. While seeking out other teams or departments to help solve *your* problems may seem counter-intuitive, I can tell you from years of experience that it can be enormously helpful. I'm reminded of a great saying attributed to author John A. Shedd: "A ship in harbor is safe—but that is not what ships are built for." That's not what human beings are built for, either! I encourage you to find time every day to explore, experiment, play, and make zany, unusual connections.

Sir Paul Goes to Number One

In 2018, Paul McCartney accomplished yet another impressive feat in a career filled with them: his album, *Egypt Station*, debuted at number one on the Billboard 200. The milestone marked Sir Paul's first chart-topper in more than 36 years (since 1982's *Tug of War*, in fact). I decided to have a little fun with a *Billboard* interview with the former Beatle to see if I could draw some simple lessons from this accomplishment.

On promoting the album:

> *PM: I said to everyone originally, "Look, let's try to enjoy this. Let's not just think, 'Oh my god, we gotta go promote an album.' Let's try and think of ideas that will actually excite us. Because I think, you know, if we enjoy it, that'll kind of communicate itself and makes it less of a laborious process."*

Few things get people more engaged than doing work that is enjoyable, fulfilling, and creative. When people are genuinely excited by their work, you don't have to cajole or prod them; just provide the necessary tools and resources and get out of their way.

On performing small warmup gigs before the big tour:

> *PM: We played a little gig at Abbey Road. And it was so cool going back there. The idea was a good one. I said to my guys, "I wanna just do a little gig somewhere before we go out on the big tour. Let's do a few little gigs." So we started thinking, "Well, where would we want to go, ideally?" And that was the trick, I think. You know, instead of just saying, "Oh, we'll go anywhere, it doesn't matter, they're all the same." [We said] "No, no, let's go to Abbey Road, that'd be fun."*

Your roots are your foundation. Sometimes you must reconnect to them in order to move boldly into the future.

On the album track "Caesar Rock":

> *PM: I was so glad to put in "Caesar Rock" 'cause it's a little more experimental. It's a little bit more me goofing 'round in my home*

studio, you know. And I think that turned out OK, so that's how it got on the album.

"Goofing 'round" is good for you! You never quite know what great stuff will result. History is full of amazing advances that came about unexpectedly.

On the album's title:

> *PM: When I came up with this title, Egypt Station, I tried that out on Greg Kurstin, the main producer, and he said, "Oh, I like that, what's that about?" And I said, "Well, that's just the title of a painting." But we realized it would sound a little bit intriguing, a little bit exotic, and so we started to make the album 'round that idea of a kind of journey.*

Doing the same thing the same way every day breeds boredom, not innovation. Each week, grant your people some time to go on a "journey" in which they challenge the status quo and explore new opportunities and possibilities together. No passport required!

Django: A Study in Resilience and Innovation

Guitar legend Django Reinhardt, who passed away in 1953 at age 43, is considered a towering figure of 20th-century music and a pioneering instrumentalist. His influence can still be heard in the playing of contemporary guitarists from practically every genre. He was by all accounts the world's first true guitar hero. I want to share a fascinating aspect of Reinhardt's life and musicianship that we can all learn from whether we're musically inclined or not.

Reinhardt spent most of his youth in Romani encampments close to Paris (the Romani are commonly referred to as *Gypsies*, although that term is widely considered pejorative). When Reinhardt was a young man and developing guitarist, a candle tipped over inside the wooden caravan he and his wife lived in. The structure was engulfed within seconds. Although the two were able to reach safety, Reinhardt emerged badly burned. He received severe injuries, including to several fingers of his left hand.

"Scar tissue forced his third and fourth fingers into a permanent hook, making them useless except to finger the upper notes of some chords on the E and B strings," writes David McCarty of *Flatpicking Guitar* magazine. "For a year and a half, he fought every day to stretch burned tissues, rebuild calluses and restore muscle memory to his hand and recuperate from his other injuries." Although his fingers were permanently damaged, Reinhardt adopted a novel way of playing using only his thumb and two good fingers. It was a style that would come to define him.

Reinhardt's story contains at least two powerful lessons. The first is that no matter what challenges we may face, the will and determination to rise above them cannot be overestimated. The second lesson is that *embracing* limitations can actually lead to innovation. As McCarty writes:

> Some writers have argued that Django's physical handicap actually made him a better guitarist than had he the use of all four fingers on his fretting hand. . . . Unable to play the

linear, scale-driven lines that fall all too easily under the fingers of most guitarists, Django's limited mobility forced him to view the fingerboard more vertically than horizontally. Blessed with exceptionally large hands and long fingers . . . he had the strength and stretch to make wide intervals with just his first two fingers. He invented the use of octave runs as a soloing device on guitar, another example of taking his two-fingered limitation and making it a musical asset.

This idea of accepting and leveraging rather than bemoaning limitations is a key principle of innovation. Each of us has limitations on our ability to accomplish our work. Not enough money. Not enough time. Not enough personnel. Many years ago, I witnessed a senior leader tell new members of her staff, "You'll face the impossible here, and you'll need to figure out a way to do it." Limitations are a part of life. They're inevitable and often unavoidable.

That's why Reinhardt's example is so powerful. In the face of significant limitations, he developed a totally new way of playing rather than give up the instrument he loved. In so doing, he became not just a great guitarist but one of the greatest of all time. It's an important lesson for artists and businesses alike, especially in this day of shrinking budgets, reduced headcount, and relentless demands on our time.

Want to Drive Creativity? Improvise!

As a jazz musician, I've always believed that strengthening your ability to improvise can boost creativity whether or not you play an instrument. That's why the workshops I do on creativity and innovation always include exercises in improvisation.

I recall an article titled "Jazz improvisers score high on creativity" that caught my attention a few years ago. Scientists at Wesleyan University posed creativity challenges to 12 jazz musicians, 12 classical musicians, and 12 non-musicians, such as brainstorming uses for a paper clip. The participants then listened to three different types of chord progressions: familiar ones, some that were a bit unusual, and some that were totally unpredictable. Their brain waves were recorded with an electroencephalogram (EEG); the participants then rated how much they liked each chord progression.

Perhaps unsurprisingly, the jazz musicians demonstrated "markedly different neural sensitivity to unexpected musical stimuli" (that's PhD talk for "they preferred the unexpected progressions more than the other participants"). More importantly to organizations, this preference for the unexpected chords was "significantly correlated with behavioral measures of fluency and originality on the divergent thinking task" (that's PhD talk for "their paper clip ideas were more creative than the other participants'"). The results suggest that improvisation may not only give jazz artists a creative advantage over other kinds of musicians but that "training to be receptive to the unexpected . . . can increase creativity in general."

Does this mean you should start giving your team members jazz lessons? Probably not. But the connection between improvisation and creativity demonstrated by the study supports my long-standing belief that the more you practice improvising, the more creative (and more innovative) you are likely to be.

How will you challenge *your* team to break free of old thinking and explore new possibilities?

"SCAMPER" Your Way to Great Ideas

Considered by many one of the greatest pop songs ever written, "Good Vibrations" by the Beach Boys earned the band a Grammy nomination for Best Vocal Group Performance in 1966 and was inducted into the Grammy Hall of Fame in 1994. "Good Vibrations" was voted number one in *Mojo's* "Top 100 Records of All Time," number six on *Rolling Stone's* "500 Greatest Songs of All Time," and included in the Rock & Roll Hall of Fame's "500 Songs that Shaped Rock and Roll." According to Wikipedia, the song "is credited for having further developed the use of recording studios as a musical instrument" and for "heralding a wave of pop experimentation and the onset of psychedelic and progressive rock."

Not bad for a song inspired by Brian Wilson's mother, who told him as a child that dogs sometimes bark at people in response to their "bad vibrations."

One of the most interesting aspects of "Good Vibrations" is its use of a musical instrument commonly misidentified as a theremin (it's actually an electro-theremin, but let's not quibble). Listen for the weird, spacey "woooooEEEEEEoooooo" sound on the recording and you'll hear it.

According to engineer Chuck Britz (cited in Domenic Priore's 2005 book *Smile: The Story of Brian Wilson's Lost*

Masterpiece), "[Brian Wilson] just walked in and said, 'I have this new sound for you.' I think he must have heard the sound somewhere and loved it, and built a song around it." At the time Wilson was considering the theremin, its use was limited to soundtracks to movies like Alfred Hitchcock's *Spellbound* and low-budget horror and sci-fi films. But in a flash of inspiration, Wilson thought that its eerie, high-frequency tone would sound good on a track that also included cello, harmonica, sleigh bells, and harpsichord. And thus, a classic was born.

Wilson knew intuitively that one of the best ways to generate new ideas is to combine elements that don't typically go together. Here's a way you can leverage that same creative spirit in your own work.

"SCAMPER" is one of my favorite creativity techniques for generating new ideas. "SCAMPER" encourages experimentation and exploration through:

- **S**ubstituting
- **C**ombining
- **A**dapting
- **M**odifying
- **P**utting to other use
- **E**liminating
- **R**earranging or reversing

It's an easy and fun exercise. Try it the next time you're attempting to gain a new perspective on a problem and see what bubbles up. Even if you don't create the next great pop song, I guarantee you'll have a new perspective on whatever issue or challenge you're facing.

Innovation in the Air Tonight

If you're familiar with Phil Collins's massive hit "In the Air Tonight," you are surely familiar with the famous drum fill that is arguably the song's most memorable feature. But did you know that drum fill almost didn't happen?

Although Collins now dismisses the fill as sounding like "barking seals," he cannot deny it's arguably the most recognizable drum fill in rock. Lasting less than five seconds, it sets up the haunting final third of the song with a palpable sense of urgency and menace. But to hear Collins describe it, the inclusion of the fill was unplanned. According to Kenneth Partridge's article "Pack of Lies" on mentalfloss.com, "The original demo had the drums dropping in without fanfare. But in the studio, Collins improvised a little flourish, as drummers often do. 'We decided to keep that take, and it happened to have that drum fill in it,' Collins said. 'It's just become what I'm known for. But it was real luck.'"

From pop music to soda pop, luck often plays a surprising role in innovation. Here are some well-known examples:

- Velcro was invented by a Swiss man named George de Mestral after his dog got caught in a bush and became covered in burrs. He viewed them under a microscope and discovered tiny hooks. The rest is history.
- In 1968, 3M chemist Dr. Spencer Silver tried to invent a super-strong adhesive but ended up developing the opposite. 3M saw little use for the weak glue that resulted, but years later colleague Art Fry used it to

keep bookmarks from falling out of his church hymnal. Post-it Notes were born.

- Penicillin was invented when Sir Alexander Fleming failed to clean up his work area before going on vacation. When he returned, he noticed a fungus (*Penicillium notatum*) on some of his petri dishes. Around the fungus, no bacteria had grown. The discovery of penicillin is considered one of the most momentous in medicine.

Many innovations are unplanned, and most are initially rejected. Does your organization have systems and processes in place to capitalize on "mistakes" and lucky breaks? Or do new ideas typically fade away because nobody is quite sure what to do with them?

RHCP: Still Grooving After Four Decades

I've been a fan of the Red Hot Chili Peppers since first seeing them at Rutgers College in 1989 (I hadn't heard of them but was intrigued by their name, so I went alone. Besides, it was a free show). Since that electrifying performance, I've acquired all their albums and attended multiple concerts. It's been interesting to watch them evolve over the years, from wild and hedonistic young punks to elder statesmen of alternative rock. But while their music has changed dramatically, one thing has remained constant—their thoughtful and articulate bass player Flea (whom I referenced earlier).

I admire Flea's musicianship, but I respect his attitude toward music-making even more. He constantly stresses the importance of not becoming complacent, of cultivating an attitude where it's not only OK to challenge the status quo but encouraged.

Few of us have the same freedom to create at work as Flea. Still, it's important to bake opportunities to be creative into every workday. Start by taking a page from Flea's "rule book":

- Slow down (if only for a few minutes) to engage your "creative" brain.
- Encourage people to get out of their comfort zones.
- Remain curious and receptive to new ideas.
- Be willing to change and grow.
- Take prudent risks.
- Never stop learning.

These are the hallmarks of longevity not only for great rock bands but for great organizations as well.

Singing the Praises of One of the World's Greatest Buildings

My visit to Australia in 2016 took me to Melbourne, Sydney, Brisbane, and the Whitsunday Islands. I fed coconuts to kangaroos, played with wallabies, made friends with an emu or two, and saw some amazing sights. One of the highlights was seeing the remarkable Sydney Opera House up close—far more impressive in person than any photo can convey.

As a musician, I was awed by the legendary talent and productions that have appeared here. But it was the humble origin of the Opera House itself that truly captured my imagination. In 1956, an international competition for a national opera house design was held; 233 entries were received from 28 countries, including Australia, England, Germany, French Morocco, Iran, and Kenya. Danish architect Jørn Utzon's scheme was selected after one of the judges, who arrived late to the selection process, retrieved it from the discarded pile. According to the Opera House's own website:

> The judges recognised the inherent brilliance of Utzon's architectural scheme: "We have returned again and again to the study of these drawings and we are convinced they present a concept of an opera house which is capable of becoming one of the great buildings of the world.... Because of its very originality, it is clearly a controversial design. We are, however, absolutely convinced of its merits."

How many bold and brilliant ideas do we discard every day because they seem unworkable, impractical, or just too weird? How many times do we clip the wings of our creativity through negative self-talk or the critiques of others? How often are we content to stay the course when an opportunity to be truly daring arises?

As the poet Mary Oliver said, "Keep some room in your heart for the unimaginable." You too may end up building a masterpiece.

Embrace the Shake: How Limitations Can Boost Creativity

Recently, I was straightening up around my home when I came across a book titled *The World's Shortest Stories*. Each story in the book is comprised of just 55 words. As the introduction states, "Fifty-Five Fiction is storytelling at its very leanest, where each word is chosen with utmost care on its way to achieving its fullest effect."

Reading these quirky, amusing stories reminded me of a workshop I gave a few years ago on innovation. One of the points I made about brainstorming was that establishing limitations—as opposed to the wide-open, "blue sky" thinking typically associated with brainstorming—can actually *spur* creativity rather than hinder it.

I provided several examples, but none were more compelling than a video of artist Phil Hansen. Hansen developed a shake (the result of permanent nerve damage) in art school, which led him to drop out and leave art altogether for several years. When a neurologist advised that he "embrace the shake," Hansen returned to art and developed new ways of painting by accepting and leveraging his restrictions.

"I went home, I grabbed a pencil, and I just started letting my hand shake and shake," says Hansen, in his TED Talk "Embrace the Shake." "I was making all these scribble pictures. And even though it wasn't the kind of art that I was ultimately passionate about, it felt great. And more importantly, once I embraced the shake, I realized I could still make art. I just had to find a different approach to making the art that I wanted."

How might *you* turn limitations, constraints, and restrictions into creative gold?

You Don't Have to be Michael Jackson to Generate a "Thriller" of an Idea

Several years ago, a friend sent me an article about how Michael Jackson wrote songs: unable to read or write music, he would build each element of a track solely *with his voice*. According to "The Incredible Way Michael Wrote Music" on mjworld.net, he would come into the studio with "every note of every chord, harmony, melody, bass and even the rhythm through beatboxing" on tape. According to Jackson, "The lyrics, the strings, the chords, everything comes at the moment like a gift that is put right into your head and that's how I hear it."

One sound engineer who worked with the King of Pop said, "He would sing us an entire string arrangement, every part. . . . Had it all in his head, harmony and everything. Not just little eight bar loop ideas. He would actually sing the entire arrangement into a micro-cassette recorder complete with stops and fills."

Just like Mozart, who supposedly heard whole symphonies in his head, Jackson had a very special talent indeed. But you don't need to possess either artist's inventive genius to churn out great creative ideas yourself. In "How to inspire and promote a culture of creativity by shaking things up" at sbsonline.com, Dr. Terri Swartz of California State University, East Bay, shares a few excellent tips for inspiring and promoting a culture of creativity.

"Creative leadership is about giving people permission to dream and encouraging them to try something different," says Dr. Swartz. "You get there by shaking things up and not letting employees settle into the status quo."

What activities and behaviors foster a culture of creativity? These are some cool suggestions from Dr. Swartz:

- When appropriate, allow participants to play with simple, creative toys like LEGO, pipe cleaners, and Silly Putty during meetings. It's surprising how noodling around with such items can spur fresh insights.
- Try Google's 70-20-10 rule. At Google, technical staff were asked to spend 70 percent of their time on core activities, 20 percent of their time on secondary business pursuits, and one day each week in a different room or location to focus on new ideas. Too often, companies prohibit nontraditional work schedules that can actually inspire creative thinking.
- Don't allow naysayers to suppress new products or ideas until they're fleshed out. I call these folks "No-It-Alls." They are a promising idea's worst enemy.
- Acknowledge, encourage, and reward creative ideas from any source. People may not mind if you don't use their idea, but they'll be irritated if you don't express appreciation for their efforts.
- Recognize that allowing employees time to explore, create, and collaborate may not yield immediate financial rewards — and that's normal. Rarely do great ideas emerge fully formed. Be patient (even with seemingly

"Bad" or "Off the Wall" ideas — get it?*) and enjoy the journey!

What can *you* do to generate creative ideas?

*If you don't, these are the titles of two Michael Jackson albums.

Remembering David Bowie

I remember waking up to news that David Bowie had passed away of cancer at the age of 69 in 2017. I've always felt we throw around words like *genius*, *icon*, and *superstar* too casually, but not in Bowie's case. In the entire history of rock music, there are only a few dozen performers truly deserving of the title *legend*. Bowie is one of them.

How fitting (and strangely coincidental) that I'd had a conversation about Bowie's last album *Blackstar* with a friend shortly before Bowie died. Bowie's work always invited dialogue and debate; his cryptic lyrics, odd time signatures, unconventional arrangements, and provocative videos were the work of a keen intellect. But Bowie, for all his intellectualism, could touch the heart as well. The opening lyrics to "Heroes," for example, could be the theme song for any couple struggling through life's travails: "I, I will be king / And you, you will be queen / Though nothing, will drive them away / We can beat them, just for one day / We can be heroes, just for one day." Most poignantly, in his final single "Lazarus," Bowie sings: "This way or no way / You know I'll be free / Just like that bluebird / Now, ain't that just like me?" We now know that he was gravely ill when he wrote and recorded "Lazarus," and those words cut like a blade.

Perhaps no song in his repertoire captures the essence of the artist better than 1971's "Changes": "Ch-ch-ch-ch-changes / Turn and face the strange / Don't want to be a richer man / Just gonna have to be a different man / Time may change me / But I can't trace time."

Bowie changed — literally and figuratively — over the years more skillfully (and more interestingly) than any other rock or pop artist. From early career characters such as Ziggy Stardust and the Thin, White Duke to the fashionable elder statesman of the last decade, Bowie was never content to stand still and rest on his laurels. Like the very best artists, he was a relentless explorer and innovator. Not all of his experiments worked, but even his so-called failures reflected a restless curiosity. Henry Rollins once said admiringly of Miles Davis: "After tons of great records and tickets sold, he said, 'Now I'm going to grow my hair out and play my horn through a wah-wah pedal.' Rather than play it safe, he went on." The sentiment applies just as easily to Bowie, who certainly could have spent his career cranking out variations of his biggest hits. Fortunately for us, playing it safe was never his thing.

In the song "Starman" from the album *The Rise and Fall of Ziggy Stardust and the Spiders from Mars*, Bowie sings: "There's a starman waiting in the sky / He'd like to come and meet us / But he thinks he'd blow our minds."

Oh you did, David. You did.

The Sound of Two Hands Clapping

In 2015, I participated in an event in Philadelphia titled "Innovation as a Business Strategy." I recall leading an unrehearsed, unscripted "jam session" with five volunteers from the audience. I handed each of them an instrument (shakers, tambourine, woodblock, cowbell, and hand drum), got the audience clapping along, and engaged the participants in a short, improvised interlude while playing my saxophone. We then discussed the experience and what it illustrated about the nature of creativity and innovation.

I want to share a moment that occurred shortly before the jam session took place. When I announced to the room that I would need *everybody's* help (not just the five people performing), one young woman way in the back started clapping and dancing spontaneously. It was a gesture of pure enthusiasm and joy. We hadn't played a single note and already this young woman was getting her groove on! Her reaction was infectious; soon the entire room was clapping along to the rhythm she had initiated.

As I reflected later, I began to realize how much of our lives is scripted. We adopt patterns of thinking, speaking, eating, driving, even sleeping, and that's OK. Without habitual ways of doing things, we would rapidly become overwhelmed. And yet, I can't help but think how all this *routine* is stifling the essence of what makes us creative beings.

In an article titled "Routine: Creativity Enabler or Creativity Killer?", author Jessica Stillman suggests that a rift exists between pro-routine and anti-routine forces. Among the latter camp is a developer who states: "Routine is deadly for creativity. It's deadly for innovation and challenging design problems, too, because it hinders spontaneous decisions, random experiments, and weird ideas."

I think that's accurate. Obviously, I'm not talking about abolishing *all* routine, but I am an advocate for building time into each day to explore, experiment, and engage in brainstorming and idea exchanges with peers. From such moments can spring solutions to seemingly intractable problems, solutions that may elude us when our brains are occupied with rote tasks and mundane chores. Because of their spontaneous nature, such moments at work tend to be the ones that are the most enjoyable.

Consider stepping away from the relentless email for a few minutes and taking a walk. Listen to music. Grab coffee with a colleague. Watch a TED Talk. Visit a part of the building you never have before. Or just start clapping (with or without people around you). Break out of your routine, even for a few minutes, and see what happens.

Will you take time today to do something unplanned?

The Power of Brevity

I'll keep this short.

I was listening recently to the great jazz saxophonist Charlie "Bird" Parker and his legendary solo on the classic tune "A Night in Tunisia" (recorded for Dial Records in 1946). This particular version contains one of the most famous solo "breaks" in all of jazz.

As the website deadlikejazz.com points out:

> [W]hile Parker's solo is nothing short of brilliant, it's the short, blazing improvised cadenza with which he begins it that still stands as a challenge to anyone attempting a life in jazz. It's 8 seconds or so of blazing invention; one of those rare meetings of virtuoso technique and creative expression that feel like diamonds when one first stumbles upon one of them. This cadenza is now known as "the famous alto break" by anyone who cares about jazz in its heyday, and sends chills down through the decades like little else in the 20th century audio lexicon.

How could such a brief burst of spontaneous music continue to inspire almost 80 years after its creation?

The answer lies in its rare combination of speed, precision, boldness, and, most notably, *brevity*.

It's precisely *because* so much invention is packed into so little time that Parker's riff endures as a milestone in the development of jazz. Of course, Parker played thousands of longer solos throughout his career, almost all of them remarkable; yet it's these eight seconds — *eight seconds!* — that perhaps best represent his singular genius.

Another example of a boatload of virtuosity packed into a short timeframe is the song "Eruption" from Van Halen's 1978 self-titled debut album. In less than two minutes, guitar prodigy Edward Van Halen displays a jaw-dropping variety of novel techniques, blistering speed, and harmonic invention that is often cited as a landmark in the history of rock guitar. As with Parker's solo, the brevity of "Eruption" serves to amplify the genius on display rather than detract from it.

Both "A Night in Tunisia" and "Eruption" remind us that when it comes to creativity and innovation, an idea need not be complicated to have merit. In fact, sometimes briefer is better.

One Final Note: What I've Learned After 30 Years in Flip Like Wilson

As a bona fide "band geek" in high school, I never dreamed I would be in a band that achieved the success of Flip Like Wilson—let alone remain an active member for three decades. Being a member of Flip Like Wilson has afforded me lifelong friends and a host of incredible memories I wouldn't trade for anything.

I'd like to share with you Four Principles for Successful Living I've learned along the way. I believe they are relevant to any human endeavor, musical or not. But before I do, I'd like to thank all of the fans, club owners, managers, coaches, and promoters who contributed to our success. And of course, thank you to every member of the band, past and present, for making the journey such a blast. You guys rock!

And now for the list. . . .

Four Principles for Successful Living I've Learned After 30 Years in Flip Like Wilson

1. Stay calm and let it go.

I've met some wonderful people in the music business. I've also met some lousy people. They routinely disappoint, betray, humiliate, and aggravate. They can even lead you to question your own abilities. These people can burrow deep under your skin and into your psyche if you let them. I've reconciled to the fact that no amount of wishing, hoping, or pleading will change these people. They simply woke up on the wrong side of the crib and never looked back. Whenever I encounter these toxic individuals, I remember that how I *react* to them is always my choice. I can react with bitterness and resentment (thus internalizing their negativity) or with grace and class. Nine times out of 10, I'll choose the latter (I am only human, after all).

The most valuable real estate in the world is between our ears. We always have the power to let in or keep out the people in our life. And while we may have to work (or live) with the human equivalent of a storm cloud, never forget that the security guard who oversees our visitors' comings and goings has an enormous influence on our well-being.

How busy are you keeping your security guard?

2. The most powerful force on earth is an inspired human being.

Whenever I try to describe the feeling of performing for a pumped-up crowd, words fail me. Throughout my career in Flip Like Wilson, there were many times when audience and band connected in a way that literally left me breathless. I remember one gig at Penn State University many years ago. We had just finished playing in a packed club called the Crowbar when a skinny kid, dripping with sweat, pushed his way to the front of the stage and grasped my hand. I can still recall his face.

"You guys ROCK!" he shouted over the din. He wasn't just excited. He was *ecstatic*. You could feel the energy pouring off him in waves. Whatever he'd just experienced had apparently ignited every nerve fiber in his body. "AWESOME SHOW!" If I could have bottled and sold his enthusiasm, I'd be living on an island somewhere.

Of course, you don't have to be a musician to inspire others. Being a friend, a parent, a teacher, a coach, or a leader will do just fine. Inspiring others is the ultimate gift we can give them; when people are inspired, they overcome challenges, push through obstacles, and redefine what's possible. Inspiration is at the heart of every accomplishment, every milestone, every breakthrough. Ralph Waldo Emerson wrote, "Our chief want is someone who will inspire us to be what we know we could be."

Who out there could benefit from your inspiration today?

3. Do not go where the path may lead. Go instead where there is no path and leave a trail.

OK, so I stole that line from good ol' R. W. Emerson (again). It's one of my favorite quotes. When Flip Like Wilson was first starting out, we decided not to play the same music every other band was playing at the time. No "Jessie's Girl." No "Don't Stop Believin'" (although we let that one slip into our repertoire a few years later, much to my chagrin). No "Brown Eyed Girl." No "Sweet Caroline." All fine songs, of course, but the world didn't need one more band playing them. Instead, we learned unconventional material like "Mexican Radio" by Wall of Voodoo, "New Sensation" by INXS, "Hold Me, Thrill Me, Kiss Me, Kill Me" by U2, and a Beastie Boys medley that we still perform to this day.

The gamble paid off. It turned out many club patrons were looking for something different to enjoy with their beers and cocktails. We began to hear things like "You guys don't play the same old stuff" more frequently, and within a year our audience had grown tenfold. We began incorporating even more offbeat (no pun intended) songs into our sets by non-mainstream artists, including Fishbone, Primus, Slip-knot, Cake, Spacehog, Blur, and dozens more.

Our audiences kept growing. In the late '90s, our fan base exploded as we took advantage of the ska and swing revivals sweeping alternative radio at the time. Of course, not every unorthodox song choice worked (see #4 below), but enough did to make me a lifelong believer in following your heart, trusting your vision, and embracing nonconformity.

Are you willing to go where there is no path and leave a trail?

4. Not everything you do will be a smash hit. Deal with it.

In our zeal to learn and perform offbeat selections (see #3 above), we've experienced our fair share of bombs. Our medley of Jay-Z songs comes to mind. It took me weeks to memorize all the lyrics; we played it twice before excising it from our repertoire. An even bigger disappointment was Duran Duran's "Rio," a song I like very much. I even learned the tricky sax solo note for note! It too was met with audience apathy and unceremoniously ditched after a couple of performances. I could mention many, many more examples of songs that failed to make an impact and were subsequently jettisoned.

I once heard a football player say that he expects to score on every play. That was his mentality. I used to think the same way about our songs. I wanted every song we learned to elicit a positive response—clapping, singing, dancing, cheering, *something*. I wanted this so badly, in fact, that I got angry when a song had the opposite effect. "How dare they!" I thought. "Don't they realize how long it took to learn this?"

As I've gotten older (and hopefully more mature), I've accepted that *not every song is going to click with an audience.* Sometimes people walk off the dance floor. Sometimes they meet your hard work and good intentions with blank eyes and upturned noses. Sometimes they leave the venue altogether. If you're in a band, what matters is that you shake it off and move on to the next tune.

It's a great metaphor for life, isn't it?

How quickly do you get up after you go down?

If you've read this far, thank you. The world needs great leaders more than ever. Now go out there and be one.

Author Bio

As founder and CEO of Right Chord Leadership, Dr. Michael Brenner collaborates with leaders and teams at all levels to strengthen the essential skills needed for peak performance. He achieves this by drawing on 25 years of experience as an international leadership consultant, executive coach, keynote speaker, and educator, and more than 40 years as a professional musician. Michael's unconventional workshops, executive coaching sessions, and consulting services — grounded in the belief that "When people work in harmony, great things happen!"™ — have helped clients increase employee engagement, reduce turnover, improve customer service, and create more inclusive work environments.

Michael is the creator of the CHORDS Model™, which consists of six key "notes" all successful leaders and teams play: Communication, Harmony, Ownership, Respect, Direction, and Support. He has partnered with leading organizations in a variety of industries, including law firm Ballard Spahr, Morgan Properties, Burlington Stores, QVC, SAP,

232 ★ Strike the Right Chord

Penn Medicine, the City of Philadelphia, Children's Hospital of Philadelphia, Boeing, The Goddard School, Godiva, and the Federal Reserve Bank of Philadelphia. He has worked for several nonprofit organizations as well, including JEVS, United Way, and Habitat for Humanity.

Michael has been a featured speaker at many industry events and conferences around the world, including South Asia, Canada, and Australia. He holds a doctorate in Adult Learning and Leadership from Teachers College at Columbia University and a master's degree in Adult and Organizational Development from Temple University. He has taught courses in organizational behavior, negotiation skills, and interpersonal relations (among others) at Immaculata University, Temple University, La Salle University, Penn State University, and the Kogod School of Business at American University in Washington, DC. Additionally, Michael has completed a certificate program on neuroscience for business from MIT.

Michael currently performs in two Philadelphia-area bands. He lives in Broomall, PA, with his wife, daughter, and two adorable cats.

Acknowledgments

I would like to express my gratitude to everyone who has helped me take this book from a promising idea to a reality.

First and foremost, thanks to my wife, Subhi, and daughter, Nadhi, for your unconditional love and support. I cherish both of you more than I can express.

Thank you to my parents for being amazing role models and teaching me the value of empathy and compassion. I hope I continue to make you proud.

Thank you to my coach, Judy Weintraub of SkillBites, for guiding me through the lengthy book development and publishing process, and my editor Elizabeth Thorlton for her deft skills and keen eye.

Thank you to my friend, Dr. James Smith, who helped me see the potential of combining my love for music with my background in learning and development, leading to the creation of Right Chord Leadership.

Thanks to all the professors, teachers, and mentors throughout my academic career whose invaluable wisdom continues to guide my approach.

Thanks to my bandmates in Flip Like Wilson and The 9's for the musical adventures and brotherhood. The journey continues . . .

Thanks, also, to all my clients—past and present—for placing your trust in me and granting me the privilege of working with your organizations.

Lastly, I would like to thank you, my readers, for your interest in my work. I hope this book inspires you to do great things.

www.ingramcontent.com/pod-product-compliance
Lightning Source LLC
Chambersburg PA
CBHW071156210326
41597CB00016B/1573